CLASSIC
British
MOTORCYCLES

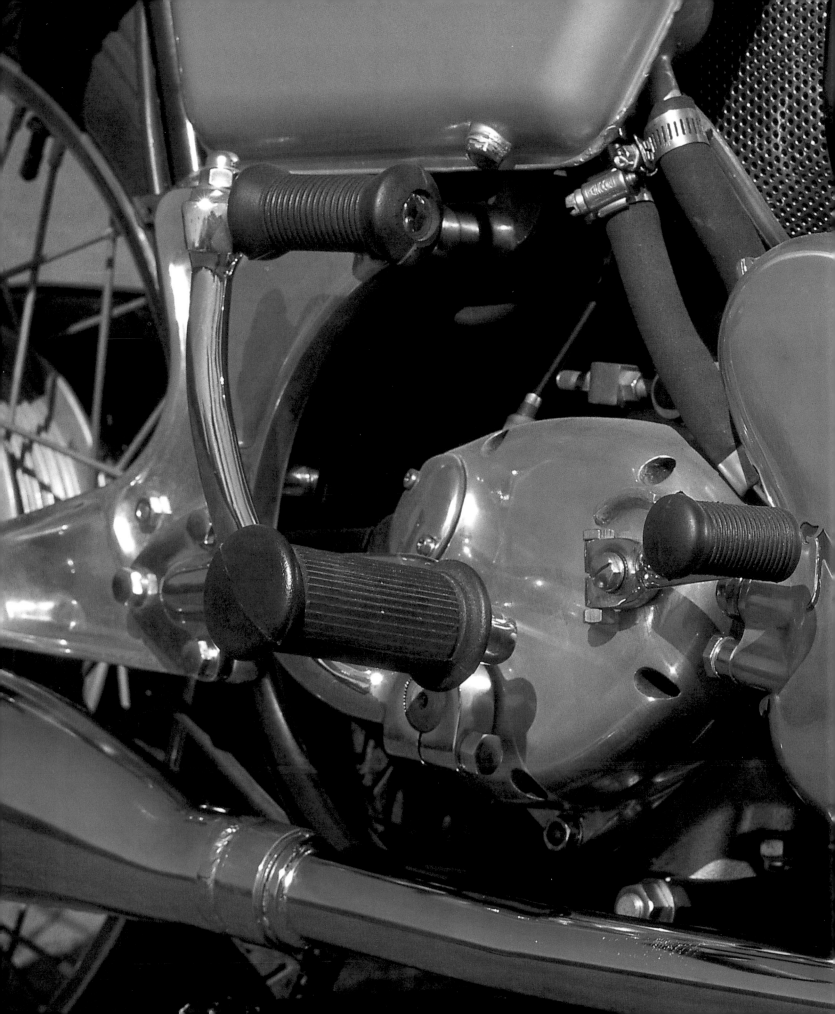

CLASSIC
British
MOTORCYCLES

·

The Cutting Edge: Fast Road Bikes 1950 to 1975

STEVE WILSON

Photographs by GARRY STUART

PUBLISHED BY
SALAMANDER BOOKS LIMITED
LONDON

A Salamander Book

Published by Salamander Books Ltd.
8 Blenheim Court
Brewery Road
London N7 9NT
United Kingdom

1 3 5 7 9 8 6 4 2

Photographs © Garry Stuart 1998
Text © Salamander Books Ltd. 1998

ISBN 0 86101 959 8

*This book is dedicated to the one I love, my wife Molly, who was also of
major technical assistance bringing the work in well fettled and on time.*

Acknowledgements
We would like to thank the following for their generosity in providing their beautiful
bikes to be photographed in this book, and in many cases also giving their time to ride
them. To John Thrussell; Ray Cook; Reg King; plus the ever-dependable Tony
Mortimer; Bill Little, purveyor of fine classics; and most especially, Don Taylor. In
addition grateful thanks to Roy Richards of the National Motorcycle Museum, and to
the Museum's Dave Roach for his brawn and good humour. Finally thanks to Cyril
Ayton, late of *Motor Cycle Sport*, for providing some of the fine period photographs.

Note
Dimensions, measurements and data in this book are presented as they were
customarily when these motorcycles were produced, i.e. in lb and inches. The 'Gallons'
quoted are Imperial not US. Production dates follow the factory system, where
production shifted to the new model year after the August of the previous year. So for
example a 'model for 1957', or a '1957 model', might actually have been built late in
1956. Weights of the machines are the dry weight unless otherwise stated, and based
on data provided by the manufacturers. Speeds unless otherwise stated (i.e. 'top speed
on test') are informed approximations of the actual top speeds which could habitually
have been expected from a production model, not flash one-way readings on machines
which might have been specially prepared by the factories for road tests.

Credits
Editor: Dennis Cove
Designer: John Heritage
Photographer: Garry Stuart
Filmset by SX Composing DTP, England
Colour reproduction by Emirates Printing Press, Dubai, UAE
Printed in Italy

Additional captions
1 The Matchless logo.
2 BSA's 1963 A10RGS Rocket Gold Star.
4 A 100mph Brooklands lap earned BSA its Gold Star.
6 The 750 Commando wore the Norton name proudly.
8 Velocette Thruxton, the last traditional single.
10 Chunky styling, big power, for BSA's Rocket 3.

CONTENTS

INTRODUCTION

FOR SPORTS ROADSTERS, the period after World War II is one of the most exciting in the whole story of motorcycling. British designs led the world, until the virtual collapse of the national industry in 1975. And leading them all, first, last and always, were Triumph twins.

Triumph's Edward Turner had stunned the two-wheeled world late in 1937 with his seminal 500cc Speed Twin (though it was originally announced as the Model T!). It was not quite the first parallel twin cylinder motorcycle produced, but it was the one that had got it overwhelmingly right. It has been said of Turner with some truth that "he knew .... what motorcyclists wanted before they knew themselves."

What they did not want was too radical a departure from the familiar, and as is well known, the compactness of the Turner twin's motor meant that it could pass for a single cylinder machine, the staple diet for riders up till then. It also meant that Triumph could use re-styled versions of the cycle parts from their existing Tiger series of singles, to house the new engine. This not only kept the new bike's weight down, it represented excellent production economy, and this kept the price down too.

For although speed is proverbially expensive, the Speed Twin was not. Really high speed roadsters up till then had been pretty much the preserve of luxury, large-capacity vee-twins by Brough Superior or Vincent–HRD of Stevenage. The latter would continue production in the glorious post-war swan-song of the form with the Series B and C Rapide and Black Shadow 1000cc vees,

Left: The 1939 Triumph Tiger 100, the progenitor of most British sports roadsters for the following thirty years. Its chromed tank and big headlamp were eye-catchers.

before the final, sensational enclosed Series D of 1955.

Triumph twins with their pushrod engines meanwhile proved as competitive on price as they were in every other department. In 1950 a 5T Speed Twin set you back £185 and change, when a traditional heavyweight single like the G80S Matchless 500 cost only a fiver less; even Triumph's sports version, the Tiger 100, was only just over £198. A Series C Black Shadow, by contrast, cost £375. This relative affordability of the parallel twins set the post-war tone. The ton-up boys and café racers of the Fifties and Sixties would be overwhelmingly working class heroes. For the other major manufacturers – BSA, Norton, AJS/Matchless, Ariel and Royal Enfield – were all compelled to follow Triumph's lead and offer their own competitively-priced parallel twins.

What was the secret of the Triumph's magic? There was universal appeal in its compactness and carefully pared weight ("Add lightness and simplicate" was a Turner dictum). The bottom line was performance; the first Tiger 100s in road trim were capable of speeds just below the magic 100mph which their name implied. Just as importantly, their power was allied to notable flexibility, so that the performance was usable in everyday conditions. And acceleration in particular seemed incredible after the heavy flywheel singles to which most riders, even sporting ones, had been accustomed up till then.

There was more. In our minds today, 'parallel twin' and 'vibration' go together like rain and public holidays, but after the jarring concussions of a tuned big single, the early Triumph twins seemed remarkably smooth. The fundamental imbalance of the 360° crank throw layout was effectively off-set by the initial small 500cc capacity, low compression and high build quality. For

years I disbelieved this, until a couple of test rides on meticulously restored early Triumph machinery impressed me with them as exceptionally smooth, by any standards. In addition, after the booming roar of a big single, the characteristic whirr of a Triumph twin with its gear-driven timing and electrics seemed positively refined.

Finally, Triumph styling offered looks which implied high performance. The low, lithe, purposeful lines of both the engine and bicycle, plus the detailing, the use of color finishes, chrome and lining, would be often imitated but never surpassed.

The Triumph's style was such that many forgave its defects in other areas, such as high-speed handling and steering, and later, front forks and electrics. But some did not (the author was one of them), and this would be one basis of the great partisan antagonisms of the Fifties and Sixties. BSA's durability and Norton's peerless handling were held up by their supporters in contrast to the Triumph engine's relatively rapid rates of wear, and their chassis' wobble and weave. But once Triumphs began to be exported to North America and used in competition there in preference to most other Brits, Yankee drive and ingenuity meant that Stateside feedback often gave Triumph the performance edge. As this book hopes to show, the actual ascendancy on the street would go back and forward for twenty-five years.

So that was the scene in 1950. With the age of post-war austerity only just beginning to recede, the major marques had a sound commercial basis in ride-to-work motorcycling. But they were also selling hard against each other to youngsters who would ride their products hard on street and track, and expect progressively hotter performance from their chosen make. Battle was truly about to be joined.

1950–1956

"ONE LUNG OR TWO?"

TWO BIKES AT THE LIGHTS, it's a Saturday night in the summer of 1956. On the inside, the snarling Shell Blue Sheen 500 Triumph, a Tiger 100 twin, near new. A quick glance shows that it carries the optional twin carburetors and big 1 gallon oil tank. Serious stuff.

But then so is the bike on the outside, one of the latest BSA Gold Star 500 singles, a DBD34 in full Clubmans trim, with dropped clip-on handlebars, rear-set folding footrests, and a shortened swept-back exhaust leading

from the tall tower of its engine to the large, shapely silencer with its deafening deep boom on fast tickover. Both machines are in the higher state of tune, with 8:1 compression, which the higher octane petrol that has

Left: A 1961 BSA DBD34 Clubmans Gold Star 500, the acme of sporting British single cylinder motorcycles.
Below: Tall gearing plus clip-on bars and rear-set rests made the Goldie uncomfortable to ride, but nearly unbeatable on the road.

come in recently allows. The riders ignore each other across the wall of noise.

The lights change and they go for it. The Triumph streaks ahead, its younger rider in his Bronx black leather jacket reveling in the incredible liveliness of the twin cylinder power delivery plus the lightest cycle parts around, going for clutchless changes, never slackening the pace because he knows what he's up against. The BSA pilot has had to slip his clutch up to 30mph, then feed in serious power and stay doggedly with the tail light

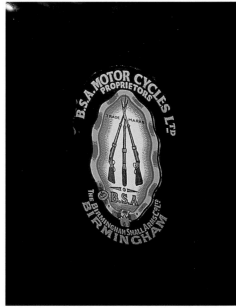

Above: *'BSA' stood for 'Birmingham Small Arms'. The giant Midlands company had started as gun-makers, and wore the 'piled arms' insignia on its side-panel decals.*

in front, smiling grimly as he sees it shimmy over the familiar tram-lines which his competition-developed frame handles rather better, though it's still a heart-stopping business. At least it's dry.

There is no traffic, the Northern town even on a Saturday night is a dead-alive desert at this hour, the few police busy with drunks. The BSA man is hitting 65 and still in 1st, making up in incredibly tall gearing for what his big single lacks in torque, reeling in the Triumph which is accelerating hard in 3rd, when the last tram lumbers up ahead of them. The single cannot afford to lose revs or power so instead of slackening pace and following the Triumph round the obstacle, he changes up into 2nd and hammers inside the lurching tram, shooting out neck and neck with the Tiger as the High Street gives way to meaner dwellings, sparsely lit by dim electric street lamps and the bikes' 6 volt headlamps. The riders' eyes

Left: *The DBD34 Gold Star's good looks were an exception to BSA's workaday image. High-mounted headlamp, chromed tank and mudguards, swept-back exhaust with flared 'twittering' silencer, and jutting GP carb were all elements in the equation.*

Right: *Gold Star specialist Eddie Dow provided this 'Duetto' twin leading shoe front brake conversion, a significant improvement on BSA's 8 inch or optional 190mm offerings.*

narrow behind MK Vlll goggles – the Goldie man wears his over a beret, the Triumph kid on his unhelmeted, Brylcreemed head – straining to read the road as it winds past the Mill and abruptly up onto the open moors.

Out on the first straight, the Triumph has hit top gear. The Gold Star is tucked in behind, tanking it, an arrow of total concentration, the crouched riding position which strained the chest and arms at town speeds now making perfect sense as the 90-mile-an-hour wind lifts the pressure from the rider's wrists, the harshness from the stiff suspension and the hammering engine forgotten in the race.

A series of wooded bends loom, tree roots adding bumps to the fast curves. The Goldie pilot muscles his machine over into the corners and is punished badly, his long forks with their rebound-only damping threatening to tangle their legs and clanging explosively as they top out, jarring his body violently and smashing his teeth together. The Triumph is even worse off, the rider feeling the frightening onset of a high speed weave at the rear as the Tiger's poorly supported swinging-arm twists and distorts. For both, the low-grip rubber of their skinny Dunlop tires is on the absolute limits of adhesion. Thank *God* it's dry.

The kid on the Triumph has the knowledge and the nerve not to back off on the throttle, but wrestling the weaving twin through on the motor takes up all the empty road and the Goldie's rider sees an opportunity on the inside and, like a bullet, takes it. As the Tiger's engine for a chilling moment misfires, the fuel frothing and surging in its carburetors' remote float chamber, the BSA man comes out ahead onto the next undulating straight, feels the quickening, unstoppable power pulses take him inexorably past the ton – and only then changes up into 4th.

Above left: *Ball-ended control levers were Fifties' luxury touches. Running the cables above the bars was an off-road dodge.*
Below left: *The Gold Star's sparse instrumentation consisted of an ammeter, and matched Smiths Chronometric speedo and rev-counter.*

Along the windswept straight he takes it gradually up to 110. Then something tells him to snap a glance behind. The Triumph's light is no longer there.

He throttles back, the big silencer 'twittering' with a mechanical chirrup on the overrun. He finds the Tiger a mile back, its headlamp unit pointing to earth, dangling from its wires where vibration has shaken the mounting screw loose and let it tumble from the shapely nacelle. The Goldie pilot fishes a screwdriver from the breast pocket of his battledress jacket, but as he takes his right hand off the throttle to hand it over, his hot engine dies. And no amount of kicking, despite the correct use of the advance/retard lever, valve lifter, choke, tickler and long swinging kick, will persuade it to life again. The two riders stare at each other. Despite these fiascos, loyalty to their chosen marques is unshaken, but they're both thinking about the same thing ...650 twins. The kid reckons that Triumph's new T110 650 would likely give him the edge over the Goldie at the top end. While the big single jockey knows that BSA's A10 Road Rocket will do just about everything he can achieve so tortuously on the Goldie – and not be such a pain to start, hot or cold.

This fictional encounter encapsulates how things stood among the fast boys as 1956 wound to a close. The traditional big sporting singles in the shape of the Gold Star had reached an apotheosis thanks to intense factory development under the spur, particularly, of the Clubmans TT races, but the DBD34 Clubman was scarcely a practical roadster, more a racer with lights. The Triumph twin in 500 semi-sports form was a good deal more tractable, lively and easy to live with, but in the crucial area of high speed handling its new-for-'54 swinging-arm frame was undeniably flawed.

Six years before in 1950, the picture had been very different. In many ways the available British sports bikes had still resembled pre-war motorcycles. Most had all-iron

Right: *Triumph's cutting-edge sportster for 1954, the pre-unit 500cc Tiger 100. Stylish and graceful, it allied light weight and a tuned 32bhp engine to produce searing acceleration. However, handling from the new swinging-arm frame was suspect.*

engines, heavier and quicker to overheat; some exceptions were the 1949 B32 and B34 Gold Stars, with their alloy heads and barrels, and Triumph's TR5 Trophy competition twin and Grand Prix racer. Part of the reason for this, and for low states of tune generally, was that the only gasoline to be had in the still-rationed UK was 72 octane 'Pool' fuel. Higher octanes sold under branded names would not be fully available until mid-1955. Ignition for larger machines was by the customary magneto, lights by dynamo, and frames were built by traditional brazed-lug construction methods, as old as the blacksmith's art.

Riders in the main still sat on sprung saddles, until the popularity of aftermarket accessory dualseats, particularly from Feridax, over the next couple of years led to their intro-

Below: *1954 Triumph Tiger 100's close-finned all-alloy engine, seen here in single carburetor form, though twin carbs were an option. Ignition was by reliable magneto, mounted behind the cylinder. Screw-on rocker box caps had a habit of spontaneous detachment.*

duction by the manufacturers. Suspension of a different kind had already come at the front end, with the widespread post-war adoption of telescopic front forks, in place of the previous girders. The best handling was provided by Norton's race-bred Roadholders, though they gave a harsh ride. AJS/Matchless Teledraulic forks were probably in second place. BSA forks, designed by Ariel's Val Page, with a version also fitted to machines from Ariel which the BSA group had owned since 1943, were strong but over-long and rebound-damped only. In performance they

tied approximately with those from Royal Enfield, though the latter were two-way damped. Bottom of the big bike league were the slim, leak-prone offerings from Triumph, with inside fork springs and long stanchions which at high speed were prone to bending and even breaking, combined with under-engineered yokes which lacked lateral support. The pursuit of lightness did have its penalties. Though progressively improved during the decade, they would remain a disadvantage until as late as 1968.

Triumph twins, like most other motor-

Above: *Triumph's headlamp nacelle, plus metal 'elbow' for throttle, helped tidy cable runs. The '4-bar' chromed tank embellishment and parcel rack were Turner touches.*

cycles in 1950, also still lacked rear suspension, unless you counted one of Edward Turner's less effective wheezes, the spring hub. This device was good for the manufacturer as it could be fitted straight into existing rigid frames, but not so good for the end user (or the user's end) as it provided only a couple of inches of movement, and affected handling adversely when worn. The same was true on all counts of the 'plunger' system of spring-boxes used by BSA and Norton at this time.

Royal Enfield, always innovative, had led the way with production swinging-arm suspension for 1949 on their sports Bullet singles, and been roundly ridiculed for it by over-conservative motorcyclists, before the benefits of the system both on- and off-road slowly sunk in. AJS/Matchless had also introduced optional swinging-arm suspension in 1949, but for years their system was to be flawed by the use of the company's own suspension units, nicknamed 'Candlesticks' and 'Jampots', with quickly deteriorating damping caused by leaks.

Among British roadsters the one, shining exception in this department of engineering

Above: *Its twinseat, shapely but effective mudguard and rear chainguard, together with full rear suspension, made the 1954 T100 practical as well as a competitive roadburner.*

as in most others was the big Vincent vee-twin, the 1000cc Series B and Series C Rapide and Black Shadow. Their triangulated rear suspension system had been effectively laid out by Philip Vincent in 1927, a cantilever design with twinned spring units positioned near-horizontally beneath the saddle – a layout the Japanese would not be

emulating right up until the early 1980s.

The majority of Vincents produced were Series C twins, and their front ends were equally unorthodox, consisting of the company's own Girdraulic forks. (Series Bs had fitted lighter, bought-in Brampton forks.) Two very strong alloy blades were the Girdraulic's main feature, with forged steel yokes providing the movement via unusually long springs in telescopic cases mounted between the crown lug and the fork end. Damping was taken care of by the Vincent's own shock absorber unit mounted centrally below the fork crown, like a girder fork's spring. The intention had been to combine the constant wheelbase provided by a girder fork with the softer action of hydraulically damped telescopics, and a further bonus was the Girdraulic's complete absence of dive

Below: *Triumph's streamlined headlamp nacelle housed the steering damper, ammeter, cut-out button, light switch and 'Rev-o-lator' speedo, as well as tidying cable runs.*

Above: *Triumph handlebars were a unique 1 inch in diameter. Seen here is horn/dipswitch, and advance/retard lever for magneto ignition on the sporting 1954 Tiger 100.*

Right: *Triumph's 8 inch single leading shoe brake, with airscoop and rear vent for the 1954 Tiger 100. This is from later on, as 1954's alone had a wavy drum side spoke flange.*

Right: *1949 Vincent Series C Black Shadow, sports version of the 1000cc vee-twins. With engines selectively assembled, plus high bottom gear, raised compression and larger carbs than the basic Rapide, the Shadow 'eliminated distance with contemptuous ease'.*

under braking. When well maintained these heavy but strong forks provided precise steering, in an accident invariably inflicted more damage than they suffered, and formed a powerful part of the unique Vincent equation.

The all-alloy 50° vee-twin pushrod motor, its gearbox built in unit with it, was as impressive as the bicycle, and indeed was integral to it. Its massive, internally-webbed crankcase was part of the structural whole, standing in for a conventional frame downtube and cradle. In the same way, the upper frame beam doubled up as the oil tank. Stung by throws at the pre-war Series A twin as 'the plumber's nightmare', the post-war twins were exceptionally clean externally, with all

Below: *Until the early Fifties Vincents were badged 'Vincent–HRD'. They bought the HRD name from Howard Davies, a Twenties TT winner, so Vincent's radical product would not seem too unfamiliar. The name was abandoned as Americans were mistaking 'HRD' for 'H–D'!*

Above: *Vincent's unique, highly advanced cantilever rear suspension system, with twin damper units positioned near-horizontally beneath the dualseat.*

oilways internal drillings, and the only external pipes being those running to and from the oil pump within. Also internally there were double guides for the valves, three row roller big end bearings, and a unique self-servo action clutch, with a conventional but light clutch transmitting initial power but also operating a drum clutch, like

a drum brake, to handle power as it rose.

Rapide versions produced 45bhp and a top speed around 110, while the truly legendary Black Shadow sports variants made 55bhp at 5,700rpm and were good for at least ten miles an hour more, making it, as claimed, the world's fastest production motorcycle at that time and for years to

Below: *Rust-proof stainless steel was used for the business-like pivot on the hinged rear mudguard, to assist in the rapid removal of the rear wheel.*

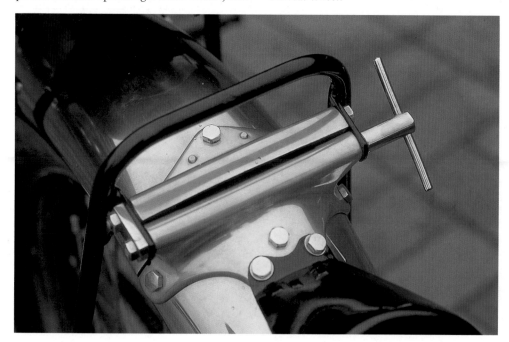

Below: *The magnificent baked-on black finish for the Shadow's engine/gearbox unit provided wonderful emphasis for its chrome, alloy and stainless steel fitments. The engine itself formed an integral part of the chassis – excellent engineering, as well as a useful weightsaver for the 458lb Series C twin. Note also the fully adjustable controls.*

come. The Shadow's superiority over the 'Rap' was achieved by a slightly higher compression ratio (but it was still only 7.3:1), bigger bore (1¾ inch) Amal carbs, polished internals, but above all, selective assembly of components which, given the Vincent company's faltering finances and hence generally antiquated production methods, could vary

quite markedly, with later bikes tending to be less rapid as machinery wore out. The Shadow's external trademarks were a baked-on heat-dispersant black finish for its engine and finning, which set off perfectly its short, splayed stainless steel pushrod tubes and the bulging knuckles of its big domed hexagonal alloy rocker-cap nuts, embossed

with the Vincent–HRD name; and a very large and prominent 5 inch diameter Smiths speedometer, calibrated to 150mph. Say no more.

Vincent, however, were at pains to emphasize that even the Black Shadow was "a tractable sports model NOT a super sports or racing machine." (They did, how-

ever, make a handful of Black Lightning full-house racers.) And unlike a racer-with-lights, the Shadow bristled with carefully thought out, rider-friendly features. The rear wheel could be removed quickly (35 seconds) and without any tools, thanks in part to a stainless steel Tommy bar spindle and a hinged rear mudguard with a substantial stainless steel pivot. Double propstands at the front could be used either separately, or together to form a center stand. All the controls were very adjustable, the foot levers being drilled for that purpose. Cables had double-wound outer casings. Wheel spokes reversed the norm and were laced into the hub, thus relieving tension on the brake drum. Both the ingenious doubling up of the engine and frame and the extensive use of aircraft-specification light alloy meant that the Black Shadow's dry weight was 458lb, which made it heavy for its day (a '54 Tiger 100 weighed 80lb less) but not unusably so, and phenomenally light and compact (the wheelbase was just 56 inches) both in view of its performance, and in modern terms.

Vincents were only ever available in small numbers, with just around 11,000 being

Below: Possibly the greatest sports roadster of all time, the low, purposeful lines of the Series C Black Shadow speak volumes about it. The semi-sprung dualseat meant that a passenger could also enjoy its effortless mile-eating.

produced in the ten post-war years, a figure considerably less than an average single year of Triumph production at that time. As noted, the twins cost roughly twice as much as other sports roadsters. But you got what you paid for. These were machines which could cruise effortlessly and tirelessly, on half throttle and little more than 3,500rpm, at 100mph which was barely within the reach of most of the competition, and then only for short periods. Everywhere you looked on a Vincent twin, it would be found to set the standard. The mighty all-alloy vee-engine was built in unit with its gearbox; a comfortable Feridax dualseat, cleverly semi-sprung, was fitted as standard; and the back-to-back 7 inch 'duo' brakes offered phenomenal stopping power for their day. These motorcycles were, as their publicity put it, "built up to a standard, not down to a price."

Philip Vincent's ideal had always been to produce the ultimate Grand Tourer, a two-wheeled Bentley Continental, with rider comfort as important as sheer performance. With the aid of his Australian design collaborator Phil Irving he came close to achieving this. Naturally the 'snarling beasts' did also compete, though most top-line road racing at that time was subject to a 500cc upper limit. The Vincent twins' forte therefore tended to be record-breaking (unsupercharged motorcycle world record in 1948 at

Above: The diminutive tail light may not have been the most practical fitment – but it was usually all that opposition motorcycles saw of a Vincent Black Shadow.

150.313mph, outright motorcycle world speed records both sidecar and solo in 1954–55 at 155 and 162mph respectively), as well as sprinting. And, of course, street-racing. The obvious targets, in the USA and Australia, were the other big vees favored there, in particular Harley–Davidsons. Standard Operating Procedure seems to have been to lay a wager, let What Made Milwaukee Famous hit its maximum speed – and then change up into top and walk away to the Shadow's 120mph-plus outer limits.

The Vincent twin was a legend in its own lifetime, and like all such legends, it could not be as perfect as its mystique implied. It could be difficult to start; not for nothing did the final, enclosed Series D shift to coil ignition. Plugs could oil up in traffic. The clever self-servo clutch was too easily contaminated with oil; clutch slip was the commonest complaint among riders, with one partial solution being to drill holes at the base of its housing to let the oil out! Even when working well, clutch engagement could be unpredictable and abrupt.

The 'duo' brakes absolutely required correct adjustment, and were not great performers in the wet. The engine was undeniably complex, the timing chest housing a complicated host of cam and gear spindles, and the engine-shaft shock absorber featuring dozens of tiny vulnerable springs. If the variations in component fit brought grief – the crank webs, for instance, could turn on the big end pin if their interference fit was not up to standard – the resulting remedial work was neither as simple for the home mechanic to undertake, nor as relatively inexpensive, as rebuilding a Triumph twin.

Finally, Vincent's pet triangulated rear suspension system and stiff Girdraulic front end were arguably showing their age by the early Fifties. One respected Clubman described the Series C roadster's cornering on bumpy bends as featuring "an action rather like a racing camel", and while the big Vin's effortless superiority on fast open roads was unquestionable, a determined

adversary could catch and out-corner them on roundabouts and tight bends.

But a Vincent's strengths far exceeded these qualifications. The exemplary smoothness of the 50° vee engine with its hypnotically off-beat exhaust note, the high speed stability, the combination of terrific torque with an equal ability to rev at high speeds, the practical accomplishment of pulling and handling as well two-up and laden as they did solo, the built-in reserves of power and

Below: *The 5 inch Smiths 150mph speedometer was the Black Shadow's trademark, and often found fitted aspirationally to Touring and Rapide twins. The second filler cap on the tank was for oil, which lived in the frame beam member under the petrol tank.*

stamina from the deliberately over-engineered motor – these made for a usable sports roadster several decades ahead of its time, a real King of the Road.

After the glorious quixotic swan-song of the final, much-modified Series D all-enclosed models for 1955, the company called it quits. Vincent twins remained, then and to this day, as an ultimate. Like their reputedly rather stand-offish riders, they tended to arouse admiration rather than warmth, even among some of those who rode them. One who owned a Series C in the Sixties wrote that Vincents "commanded respect for technical excellence while failing to inspire the affection that demonstrably inferior bikes – like for example, a Triumph twin – could so easily manage." Yet just by

being there in the background, for British bike enthusiasts they hover like some distant aristocratic relation, whose company you might not permanently relish, but whose mere existence is an absolute backstop for the family honor.

At the other end of the scale from the posh Vincent was BSA's Gold Star, a real working class hero. The model grew out of the company's humble commuting B31 350 and B33 500 singles, though these provided an excellently robust basis. It was also ironic that BSA should come up with such an outstandingly competitive motorcycle, as they had sworn off Grand Prix road racing after a disastrous TT entry back in 1921.

But they had not rejected Trials and scrambles, which is what the original postwar B32 and B34 machines were designed for. They had the advantage of a virtually bomb-proof bottom end and a reliable double-gear oil pump, laid down by the underrated Val Page before he had left to work at Ariel. But the BSA singles were heavy, so the move to lighter, heat-dispersant alloy for the heads and barrels of competition bikes was no formality; the weight-saving on the engine alone was around 20lb. From 1949 the first 350 alloy-engined comp bikes were offered, bearing the Gold Star name. This commemorated the Brooklands Gold Star given in 1937 for a 100-mile-an-hour lap of the Surrey circuit on a tuned BSA Empire Star, which had been the moment when the company had started hotting up their singles. But the Star system also pre-dated that, as the factory used to stencil a star on the crankcase to identify a customer's works-tuned machine.

One of BSA's top competition riders was Irishman Bill Nicholson, a versatile winner at scrambles and road racing as well as the more popular Trials, and also a talented development engineer. In Ireland Nicholson had been friendly with Ulstermen Rex and Cromie McCandless. The brothers were working on rear-sprung motorcycle chassis,

Above left: *Dual 7 inch brakes on the Vincent twins' rear end, and stainless steel Tommy bar to aid wheel removal without tools.*
Left: *Vincent 'duo' back-to-back 7 inch front brakes were excellent stoppers when correctly adjusted halting from 30mph in 26 feet.*

which as we shall see would come to fruition in Norton's benchmark Featherbed frame. But Nicholson also worked closely with them to graft versions of their system to experimental BSA singles, for road racing and for scrambles; he also modified the BSA front end, and eventually persuaded the management to adopt his all-welded, duplex-downtube swinging-arm frame with a wraparound steering head gusset for the production Gold Stars for 1953, a benefit which would pass (but without the gusset) to the roadster twins the following year. The Featherbed might be the boss but the BSA frame was a worthy runner-up, and also much more durable off-road.

BSA, the Giant of Small Heath, might have been averse to pure international road racing, but after the war there was one aspect of it they could see the point of, where the regulations restricted competitors (in theory at least) to production machinery, so that victory directly encouraged sales. The Clubmans TT on the hallowed Isle of Man was the post-war showcase production event for amateurs, and when one of the new 1949 Gold Stars won the Junior race, the company threw its considerable weight into the event. Like all other manufacturers, BSA bent the rules a little. Production Gold Star frames, for instance, were made of standard steel tubing, but those of favored entrants would sometimes be crafted in the specially light and strong Reynolds 531, with their steering heads dropped a couple of inches and the forks shortened to suit.

350 Gold Stars won the Junior Clubmans TT every year from then on, beating overhead cam KSS Velocettes and Norton Internationals, and forging a legend of speed and reliability. To achieve this meant continuous development, and an additional spur to it was the fact that in the increasingly important American market, the requirements of AMA Class 'C' racing, which included the Daytona Beach races, were much the same as for the Clubmans TT.

Right: *Superb 1961 500 Gold Star, with Amal GP carburetor's bellmouth defiantly unfiltered. At rest, some owners sealed this gaping orifice with a bath-plug to prevent ingress of large foreign bodies! The finned tappet cover is a Dow aftermarket goodie.*

At Small Heath's Development Dept. under the great designer Bert Hopwood, the ultra-versatile Gold Star engine, already cleaning up in works hands at Trials and scrambling, was patiently worked at to extract more power for the tarmac. There was improved breathing and valves and a shortened con rod for 1952, with the swinging-arm frame and a better gearbox off Hopwood's A7 twin for the BB series for 1953. Most of the engine development concentrated on the 350. The reason for this has only recently emerged; for the 500 class, BSA management had decreed that efforts should center on an all-alloy version of the A7 twin, hoping to match Triumph's Tiger l00s. However, their twin had proved fragile at racing speeds, and for 1954 Hopwood was able to persuade his bosses that since they were already spending money doing a new, massively finned cylinder head for the 350 Goldie, it would not cost much more to do one for the 500.

This was the breakthrough. In 1954 CB form, fitting the big head with square-shaped fins now enclosing the pushrod tunnels, rocker adjustment by a lighter eccentric spindle method, revised engine breathing and an Amal GP carb, the con rod shortened again and with the 500's flywheels made oval to suit this, the CB34 500 won the Senior Clubmans for the first time, and versions of the 500 also took 3rd, 4th and 5th at Daytona behind a pair of A7s. 1955 saw the penultimate DB series, with shorter piston skirts permitting round flywheels again, plus a swept-back exhaust. The Senior Clubmans was won by Eddie Dow. He went on to win the inaugural Thruxton 9 hour race, to which the focus of UK production racing would shift after 1956; that was the final year for the Clubmans TT on the Isle of Man, at least partly because the entry for the event was now almost entirely made up of Gold Stars.

That year's DBD34 series, with a bigger 1½ inch GP carb, 'twittering' silencer,

Right: *Top rider Arthur Lampkin aviating a late works swinging-arm B34 Gold Star scrambler. Trials and scrambles played a crucial part in the development of the model, particularly in the hands of Bill Nicholson. This made Goldies the great all-rounders.*

RRT2 close ratio gearbox and 190mm front brake, proved the swan-song. By then the best racing 350s were producing 35bhp, with the 500s in full race form seeing an impressive 44bhp – the same as the latest Manx Norton racers. The ultimate power came from higher revs, achieved by the larger carburetor, higher compression, light valve gear and better valve springs, and sustained by cooler running from the big fin alloy heads as well as from higher octane fuel.

At that point a kind of reverse takeover at boardroom level then put Edward Turner from Triumph in charge of BSA's Automotive division, and Turner felt that singles were outmoded – he believed in twins, and specifically his own Triumph twins. His commercial instincts were probably, as usual, correct; sales of the well-liked B31 350 roadster peaked in 1955, and declined steadily thereafter. At any rate, Gold Star development was stopped dead, though production lingered until 1963, largely under demand from the sports-oriented USA, where the Goldie's robust nature was well appreciated. In one aspect the Gold Star was the victim of its own success. In the first years, to at least 1954, they had their own assembly line, staffed and manned by dedicated, knowledgeable experts who had

hand-built them. When demand meant that production shifted to the regular assembly line, quality suffered.

But despite the development dead end, in Britain as well as America, the cult of the Gold Star had taken hold. And though Goldies could be had in Touring as well as competition specification, this cult, which peaked around 1960, centred on the Clubmans DBD34, the 500. Several mature and reflective riders have declared that the 350 was actually a pleasanter machine, more tractable at low revs, faster through the gears, etc. But the fast crowd would have none of it – some road test 350s had been pushed to make 90mph, and up against 500 and 650 twins on a big single, you needed everything you could get. The axis of this cult was a shop, Eddie Dow's Gold Star Centre in Banbury, Oxfordshire.

Above: *The DBD34 Clubman Gold Star's low clip-on handlebars were a pain in the wrists in traffic, but made sense tonning-up on the by-pass.*

There were solid benefits, in both top speed and strength, to the race-bred DBD 34's engine and frame, but there were several penalty clauses also. Starting was more than a knack, especially if you upped the compression with a Dow 10:1 slipper piston. One culprit was the Lucas Magdyno, when a racing mag would have produced a more useful output, but in this as in other aspects, BSA management wanted to keep the Goldie in line with their standard roadsters. This also contributed to a relatively high machine weight; over 30lb lighter than a cooking B33, but still heavy for a sporting single at around 385lb dry. The BSA 'dry' 6-spring clutch was not the best, prone to both slip and drag. The close ratio RRT2 gearbox with its so-tall 1st gear was not too practical in traffic, since it meant that the flawed clutch had to be slipped to anything up to 60mph, and the same went for the racing GP carb which

Left: *Capt. Eddie Dow, later the guru of the Gold Star cult, giving 110 per cent on a 500 in the 1953 Senior Clubmans TT, before retiring on the third lap. The previous year he had broken Geoff Duke's lap record, but then crashed at Laurel Bank. In 1955 he won.*

would not (and was never intended to) tick over in traffic.

On the road, the late 500s vibrated, possibly because their round flywheels were simply the oval ones, turned down. The riding position inflicted by the obligatory clip-on handlebars and rear-set footrests was a wrist-straining pain in traffic. The lack of torque low down meant that revs were important and had to be husbanded, but conversely, over-revving, past the 6,800 red-line through the gears, had to be watched, as it wore the engine quickly.

Steering needed firm muscular input. The over-long fork legs dictated by a relatively high steering head were a weak point, with the original strong steel mudguards and their stays acting as a very necessary brace. Rebound-damped only, the forks would bottom out alarmingly at speed on bumpy road surfaces. A cure existed in the shape of Dow's 'Superleggera' two-way damping kit, but even that restricted the 3½ inches of fork movement by a vital inch, and would

shake the rider up badly on poor surfaces. The optional 190mm front brake was another dubious benefit. The 500s ridden hard would rarely hold their tune for more than 5,000 miles, and were maintenance intensive. The ultimate Achilles' heel was the roadster-based built-up crankshaft, which was stressed at prolonged racing speeds.

No one, however, could deny the Goldie's charisma. The swinging-arm models' chrome and matt silver petrol tank, lined in Post Office Red and with its unique big round red badges, was a crowning glory on a well-proportioned machine. The Gold Star experience may have been a brutal one, the ride rough, mostly uncomfortable and very noisy, but mastering one brought undeniable satisfaction. On an

open road when everything chimed and the thundering big single carried you like God's own hammer inexorably, endlessly toward a potential 115mph top end, there was nothing to match it, and few to catch it.

Unlike the giant BSA group with its diversified interests – guns, cars, machine tools, etc – Triumph did one thing – make motorcycles, and apart from the 200cc Tiger Cub tiddlers, big twin cylinder motorcycles. Though like the Goldie at first, in this era they concentrated on a smaller capacity as their sports bike. Partly this was because most European competition was limited to 500cc, while in America the patriotic AMA often imposed that limit on imported Limey bikes against home-grown 750 side-valve vee-twins. And partly it was because Triumph's first post-war 650, the 6T Thunderbird introduced for 1950, was deliberately a soft-tuned iron-engined tourer – the Americans dubbed the first version "the cast-iron snail", before the 6Ts had quickly been fitted with a larger single carburetor.

Below: *The new-for-1954 Triumph swinging-arm frame brought a new compactness to the handsome Tiger 100 models. Blue was the archetypal Triumph color, with its Coventry connections (originally a blue derived from the town's medieval process of felting wool).*

Left: *The pre-unit Triumph's swept-back lines were cleverly designed to "look as if they were doing 100mph even when they were standing still." The parcel rack was practical, but it concealed the company's decision to discontinue chromed tanks.*

At Triumph's Meriden factory, competitive twins had to be crafted practically in secret, as Edward Turner, who had survived the Depression, kept his eyes on reliability, economy and above all cost-effectiveness and profitability, and did not consider that racing contributed much to the latter. "Prestige is all very well," he would say, "if you can afford it." Nevertheless, in Experimental and in 'Baker's Corner', the tiny product development section, unofficial racing machinery was put together. Vital input on big valve heads, hot cams and their followers, and the higher compression which the higher octane gas permitted, came from Triumph's USA organizations, the East Coast's Dennis McCormack and his top tuner Rod Coates, plus their West Coast equivalent Pete Colman, because in America the accepted principle was 'Win on Sunday, Sell on Monday', so competition was positively promoted.

Triumph's twin cylinder engine had a lot going for it. Its gear-driven camshafts, positioned fore and aft of the cylinders, meant that by varying the camshaft mix, it could be infinitely versatile, excelling as anything from a 350 Trials iron to a 650 roadburner. The pushrod cover tubes did obscure air flow to the engine, and particularly the air flow over the cylinder head, which was something that made cooler-running alloy components particularly valuable for a Triumph. The hemispherical cylinder head with valves set at 90° was a sound design, though the deep chambers and wide valve angles were ultimately limiting factors to performance.

The 'wet' clutch was superior to its BSA equivalent, and the 4-speed gearbox, separate, or 'pre-unit' as opposed to the later designs with the engine and gearbox enclosed together, was strong and pleasant to use. The three-piece bolted-up crankshaft, initially running on a caged ball race on the drive side and a double-lipped roller race on the timing side, set a natural advisable ceiling to revs ("never go more than 7") and was a limiting factor at racing speeds – but a Tiger 100 would still win the prestigious Senior Clubmans TT in 1952.

A further potential weak spot was the double-plunger oil pump, which in the absence of efficient oil filtration was a design vulnerable to dirt which could score the bores, cause non-return valve balls to fail to seat, and eventually stop the pump working. But low warranty claims on both sides of the Atlantic indicated that Fifties' Triumph twins were by and large not overstressed. Electrics at the start were by dependable rearward-mounted magneto with simple wiring, and less efficient forward-mounted dynamo for the lights. A bonus for machines so equipped was a most effective crankshaft shock absorber, a big factor in the exemplary smoothness for which, in contrast to later times, Triumph engines were still famous in this era. When the touring models went over to the more economical but less reliable crankshaft-mounted alternator for their electrics from the mid-Fifties, the rubber-segmented clutch shock-absorber which then

had to replace the crankshaft one was both less effective, and reduced rear chain life.

Triumph's style was a big factor in their appeal. An audacious move for 1949 had been grouping all the instruments previously found in a tank-top panel into a shapely headlamp 'nacelle'. The tank-top space where the instruments had been was filled by another Triumph trademark, a chromed tank-top parcel grille. The nacelle held the distinctive 'Rev-o-Lator' speedo, with four concentric scales in its dial to indicate approximate rpm through each gear (though hats off to anyone who had time to peer at it when a Triumph was accelerating hard!). In contrast to pre-war models, Turner had dropped chromed petrol tanks,

Below: *The Triumph's fore and aft layout for its twin camshafts made for a pleasingly symmetrical engine. The joints of the two separate bolted-on rocker-boxes were known for oil leaks.*

reportedly after trouble with the trade unions in the plating shop. "From now on," he declared, "we shall stove-enamel our tanks, and we shall design a motif to provide the glitter." This he did, first in the shape of the four-band chrome tank embellishment containing the Triumph logo badge. From the curved chrome surround of the front number plate, to the slim bridge to the rear number plate which doubled as a lifting handle, stylishness abounded. Triumphs sat light and graceful, their pullback handlebars complementing the streamlined nacelle to give a sense of fast forward movement even at rest.

The company's first post-war sports 500 had been the fast but extremely fragile purpose-built racer, the Grand Prix, which had featured alloy barrels derived from a wartime generator set. When this was discontinued after 1950, the 1951 Tiger 100 sports roadster became a substitute for it. This was achieved in two ways. Firstly, all

T100s were fitted with new die-cast alloy cylinder heads and barrels, with close pitch fins; the head was also finned, with larger inlet valves and splayed exhaust ports. The previous iron-engined T100s had been down on acceleration compared to the pre-war versions due to lower compression because of the 'Pool' fuel, and the new alloy-engined models remedied this, and weighed in at just 365lbs dry. Already catalogued as having polished engine internals, and with a stock compression of 7.8:1, the alloy T100, tested at 92mph, was the fastest standard roadster 500 twin available, with power up from 30 to the pre-war 32bhp.

And secondly, from 1951 they could be

Right: The plastic Norton 'quadrant' tank badges were new for 1955 but the 'curly Norton' logo dated back to Edwardian days. Below: The 1955 Dominator 88 500 twin in its state-of-the-art Featherbed frame was as handsome as it was effective.

some 13mph faster in T100C form. The 'C' stood for 'Convertible', and involved the optional use of a £35 Race Kit – which Turner liked, as it carried no warranty liability. Its principal feature, for the first time on a Triumph roadster, was something that would be a prime go-faster badge for the next twenty years, namely a cylinder head carrying twin carburetors, in this case Amal Type 6s with remote float chambers, mounted on parallel inlet ports.

Twin carbs on their own offered little extra performance. What they permitted, as the Americans had already discovered, was wilder valve timing, which really did mean superior cylinder filling and gas flow. Accompanied in the kit by hotter cams and followers, high compression pistons, stronger valve springs, a rev counter, racing exhaust system, etc, in full race form the T100C was good for 40bhp and was quite competitive in the '51–'53 era before the 500 Gold Star had been developed. Though really

only on short circuits, as the extra power, despite the adoption of the 6T's stronger con rods and clutch, overstressed the roadster crankshaft and exposed the borderline handling. For 1953 only, the T100C was offered as a complete production package fitted with all the equipment, including the first of the famous E3134 ultra-sporting cam profiles. Then it was all change.

For with BSA's swinging-arm frame going on offer for their roadsters, Triumph now produced one of their own. By compressing the engine, the new frame's wheelbase at $55^3/4$ inches was less than an inch more than that of the rigid chassis. It was still a brazed cradle, single downtube design, but now with a swinging-arm pivoting on the saddle tube, controlled by Girling three-position units. Unfortunately, as is well known, the swinging-arm, unbraced to the frame, turned the saddle tube into a torsion bar and led to the Triumph frames being known as 'Instant Whip'. If anyone doubted this, at the races they could watch Triumph rear ends visibly flexing. This weak swinging-arm came in conjunction with a long, under-braced steering head tube to suit revised front forks.

In addition, however, '54-on machines featured usefully strengthened engines with stronger con rods again, and a thicker 'big bearing' crankshaft, again off a 650, the new T110, with the main bearings now including a timing side single ball journal to replace the previous roller bearing. Other benefits were an overdue increase in front brake size to 8 inches, more comfortable twinseats, and characteristic 'Teardrop' silencers which gave a lovely throaty exhaust note.

At normal road speeds the handling problems were not chronic, and for the fast boys the limits of the new frame's handling were at least predictable, and techniques could be learned to take it to those limits. Over the years the front forks were progressively improved. Among compensations was a relatively light machine, at 385lb dry some 33lb lighter than the equivalent BSA A7SS

Right: *The Norton Dominator 88 for 1955 featured a Featherbed frame, now with its rear sub-frame welded rather than bolted on. A new cylinder head in alloy brought tuning potential. Detail changes included the first Amal Monobloc carburetor.*

model, and one with phenomenal acceleration. A 1957 T100, which came for that year with an optional 9:1 compression twin carb head based on the 650's and fitting Amal Monoblocs on splayed inlets, went from 0–60 in just 5 seconds, when the A7SS took 8. This T100's top speed was 105mph.

That was the last year at the leading edge for the Tiger 100, which would be phased out in late '58 in favor of a tamer unit construction 500 successor. As mentioned, 1954 had seen the first sports 650, the T110, which was to evolve unevenly but inexorably into the Bonneville. But for a time the alloy-engined T100 had been the hot roadster. Despite its negative points, the pre-unit 500 is remembered unfailingly with affection. It was cheap to buy, maintain and soup up, and in plentiful supply in contrast to the expensive Norton equivalent.

Norton, a name synonymous with racing, had a 500 twin which had started life in 1949, its design the work of the late, great Bert Hopwood. Hopwood had worked under Turner in the development of the Triumph parallel twin, and with his own version intended to avoid some of the drawbacks on that of his ex-boss. He placed a single four-lobe camshaft in front of the cylinder, with pushrod tunnels cast into the cylinder block to get round the obstruction of Turner's forward-mounted exterior pushrod tube. Also to help cooling, the exhaust valves were splayed and the exhaust ports, with finning around them encouraging the flow of cooling air between exhaust and inlet ports, were set wide apart; the splayed exhausts would be a Norton twin trademark. The inlet ports were placed close together, and this dictated until 1958 that the Norton would be a single carb engine. However, the combustion chamber was shallow and the valves steeply angled, and Nortons would be the best-breathing twins of them all.

Chain drive for the single camshaft and the rear-mounted magneto was to dodge the equivalent Triumph gear-drive, which Hopwood believed condemned it to be "fun-

Left: *The 1955 Dominator 88 featured full-width hubs front and rear, and the sliders on its Roadholder front forks were now polished and not enameled.*

damentally a rattler". Production economy meant that the engine was to be all-iron until 1955. Perhaps partly for compactness, to help it fit into the existing cycle parts of Norton's ES2 single, the twin had a shortish 72.6mm stroke, in contrast to the 80mm of the 500 Triumph. The result was a pretty tough engine, which could be ridden fast over long distances. The cycle sported the excellent if harsh 'long' Roadholder telescopic forks. The bottom end was strong and the gearbox race-proved. But with a top speed barely over 90mph, it was no more than the equivalent of the Triumph – and its cost was 10 per cent higher.

The breakthrough came for 1952, when at first for export only, the Dominator 88 was introduced, with the twin engine now in Norton's legendary race-bred frame, the Featherbed. (TT racer Harold Daniell: "It's just like riding on a Featherbed.") The Belfast-based McCandless brothers, after the association with BSA's Bill Nicholson already mentioned, had come to Norton to design a replacement frame for their Manx racers. They offered their welded, duplex-loop chassis, with the downtubes sprung into position inside the twin top rails and then welded to the headstock, to form a crossover bracing arrangement of tubing there. A rear sub-frame, bolted on until 1955 and controlled by fat Armstrong units, and a well-braced swinging-arm, completed the

Above: *Norton's 1953–1955 instrument panel was a weak point stylistically, when compared to Triumph's graceful nacelle.*
Above right: *'Bicycle pedal' footrests with the curly Norton on them were a charming (and comfortable) feature until 1957.*

package, with the petrol tank resting on top of the top rails, and well-damped, broad-set 'short' Roadholder forks at the front.

The roadster twins' version of this frame was arc-welded in 'B' grade tubing by Reynolds Tube, whose capacity apparently helped limit production to around 250 frames a week. The Fifties' versions were the so-called 'Wideline' variants, rather broad for the rider as the seat and tank necessarily had to be wider than the frame rails. The steering lock was restricted, the seat was relatively high and the suspension not soft, better when ridden two up than solo, but the plus side was a tireless engine and of course, steering and roadholding, in the words of VMCC founder C.E. 'Titch' Allen, "way ahead of anything else... a standard that became a yardstick by which other machines of the era were judged... It did not have to be put into a corner and held on line with any conscious effort. The mere transference of thought between machine and rider seemed enough..." Yet in its early versions, the 88's engine was no more than worthy. The model was conceived of by Norton as a luxury roadster (with a price tag

over 20 per cent greater than the equivalent Triumph). The company thought of the International with its Manx-derived single cylinder ohc engine as the supersportster. But the Inter was yesterday's man.

The change to sports status came, once again, thanks to pressure from America, in this case to contest Daytona. For 1955, a Daytona-developed alloy head was fitted to the production Dominators, and the engine's tuning potential began to be developed for the first time. In polychromatic gray for the teardrop panels of its chromed tank as well as the sinewy outline of its Featherbed frame, with its swelling pear-drop silencers and that year's slimmer mudguards, the '55 Dominator was also an outstandingly handsome motorcycle, only let down by a rather crude instrument panel and untidily exposed steering head.

1956 would see it joined by an enlarged version, the 600cc Model 99, and both featured alloy cylinder heads, raised compression ratios and the Daytona camshaft. Together these meant that performance began to match the handling. The engines were docile at low speeds but then came alive higher up, rewarding the rider who would use the gearbox to exploit them. The 600 was a nice enough bike, though vibratory, and just capable of the ton, flawed only by a crankshaft sometimes overstressed to breaking point by its extra 10mm stroke. But veteran Norton troubleshooter John Hudson has written "If I only had one machine, I'd have a 500cc 88. It can be... persuaded to go very quickly." So as the latter half of the Fifties arrived and the pace on the street hotted up, Norton twins, though a minority numerically, were well in contention.

1961 Clubmans Gold Star 500

This 1961 Clubmans Gold Star 500 was virtually the same machine as when development on the model had been terminated in 1956, give or take a larger rear chain. Almost brutal good looks match its harsh, uncompromising, demanding yet rewarding character. A racer with lights, it was tailored for just one thing – speed.

Specification

Model
BSA DBD34 Clubmans Gold Star 500
Year
1961
Bore and stroke
85 x 88mm
Displacement
499cc (30.43cu. in.)
Bhp
40 @ 7,000rpm
Top speed
115mph (185kph)
Fuel consumption (overall)
40mpg
Transmission
4-speed
Wheelbase
54 inches
Wheel and tire dimensions
3.00 x 19in (front); 3.25 x 19in (rear)
Frame type
Duplex downtube cradle
Weight (dry)
383lb (173.72kg)

1956–1963

"BATTLE OF THE TWINS"

THE REMAINING YEARS of the Fifties were in many ways the peak ones for Britain's motorcycle culture. A lot of people were riding bikes, and a lot of them were younger than they had been in the past, because they could now afford two wheels. There was full employment, and by 1959 the wartime baby boom meant that there were 5 million teenagers in the UK, with a disposable income of £800 million. In 1948, only a third of all riders had been aged between 17 and 25. By 1965, over 40 per cent were actually under 21. Another statistic was less happy: through the Fifties, 30 per cent of all traffic accidents and fatalities involved two-wheelers.

With a parental generation whose ranks had been serried by the war and its social

Left: A youth icon for the post-war age. Black leather jackets were a canvas you could paint your dreams on.
Below: The 1957-on Triumph 'mouth-organ' tank badge, another rocker icon, which the leather boys sometimes wore as a belt buckle.

fallout in terms of broken homes, teenagers were soon putting together their own youth culture with the help of Gaggia espresso machines and glass cups, Elvis, Buddy Holly and the new 45 singles and EPs. Not for nothing was the seminal youth movie, released in 1956 with its star already dead on the road, titled *Rebel Without a Cause*. A prominent section of the new youth rode motorbikes, and perhaps their appearance reflected a certain moral vacuum after the savagery and courage of the World War,

which as young men they could not help looking back to.

They wore long white tasseled art-silk scarves like the iconic Battle of Britain fighter pilots, for flamboyance but also, like the pilots, to prevent a chafed neck as they twisted for 'the life-saver' look behind – café racers didn't fit mirrors. And like Royal Navy men, they wore oiled white sea-boot socks, turned over the top of their high leather boots to slow the entry of rain. And though practical protection, the menace of black leather jackets with silver zips and studs at some level in a European mind had to echo the old black and silver of the Waffen SS. Though in a still comparatively innocent age, Britain's mild ones would often dilute the effect by wearing their school ties and white shirts under the iconic black jackets. Crash helmets were not compulsory, as the police had said they would be unable to enforce a helmet law, but by the late Fifties they were worn voluntarily by 50 per cent of riders – the English climate

encouraged it – and the ones the youth liked were the new Jet pilot kind.

The black leather boys were known as rockers, ambiguously referring both to rock and roll, and to the pivoted arm in their bike's valve gear. Or greasers (Castrol and/or Brylcreem). Or ton-up boys, defining the performance envelope aspired to, at a time when the average speed of a lorry was 40mph and of a family saloon, 50mph. Petrol, despite the 1956–57 hiccup of the Suez crisis, cost comfortably less than 5 shillings (25p) a gallon. There were no upper speed limits on the open roads.

Motorcycle manufacture was subject to the 'Stop-Go' measures which, to dampen or stimulate the economy, used variations in interest rates, purchase tax, and, above all, in hire purchase rates. 25 per cent of cars were bought on hire purchase schemes, but 75 per cent of two-wheelers, indicating how motorcycling was overwhelmingly a blue collar pursuit. But despite all that, as the Fifties drew to a close, registrations rose,

Above left: *The Ace Café, just north of Hanger Lane on London's North Circular by-pass, was one of the top rocker venues.*
Above right: *Lewis Leathers in London was a rocker's mecca, and the Esso dolls were much prized. But there was a darker side to the scene.*

and thanks to a dramatic pre-election h.p. cut from Prime Minister Harold 'You Never Had It So Good' Macmillan, peaked in the wonderful boom year of 1959, with 331,806 new two-wheelers sold and the following year, 1,420,000 on the road.

1959 was also the year when Triumph's sports twins came together in their definitive incarnation. The story had started in 1954 with the introduction of the T110, the first sports 650, after prototype testing on- and off-road by works rider Jim Alves in the tough 1953 ISDT (International Six Days' Trial). The 'ton-ten' was an instant hit with the coffee bar cowboys, as well as being the most popular model in America. With the 'big bearing' crank and stronger con rods, it retained a magneto for ignition. It thus avoided the problems associated with the more economical crankshaft-mounted alternators which Turner was introducing for the cooking models. Sports camshafts based on the American 'Q' profile, larger inlet valves and an 8:1 compression ratio, together boosted power to 42bhp at 6,500rpm.

The motor was still all-iron, with a single carb but a TT-pattern float chamber, and although acceleration was excellent, power delivery was harsh at low speeds. Also the sports 650's iron cylinder head soon proved an embarrassment at speed, regularly cracking between the edge of the valve seats and some of the eight holding-down studs. Overheating too became a real problem, particularly since, despite improved oil circulation, actual oil capacity in the restyled tank had dropped from 6 to 5 pints. The head distorted, causing oil leaks, blown head gaskets, and loss of power from poor combustion. Other problems with the T110 included rapid exhaust camshaft wear, gearbox oil leaks, and the high speed handling. "If you ever want to frighten yourself," wrote seasoned journalist Dave Minton, "give an early swinging-fork 650 Triumph lash around a mountain road." But they started easily, were ton-plus if not ton-ten motorcycles, and £10 cheaper than a 500 Gold Star, though the latter continued to have the edge in production racing. T110s in '55 and '56 might win the 750 class at the Thruxton 9 hour races, but they were led home in the overall results by a clutch of Goldies.

This was despite the fact that for 1956, Triumph had introduced for the T110 a new alloy cylinder head featuring cast-in air passages, and known as the 'Delta head' because of its shape. The improved cooling, plus a compression raise to 8.5:1, hoisted top speeds just short of an actual 'ton-ten'.(There had been a sensational 117mph recorded on one 1954 road test, but it has subsequently emerged that the engine had been very heavily breathed on by the factory, possibly while the journalist in question was being taken to lunch!) The head was still prone to cracking,

Right: *The 59 Club was a uniquely British phenomenon run by the rockin' Reverend Bill Shergood. Sweet Gene Vincent got his limp from a '53 bike smash, and wore the leathers.*

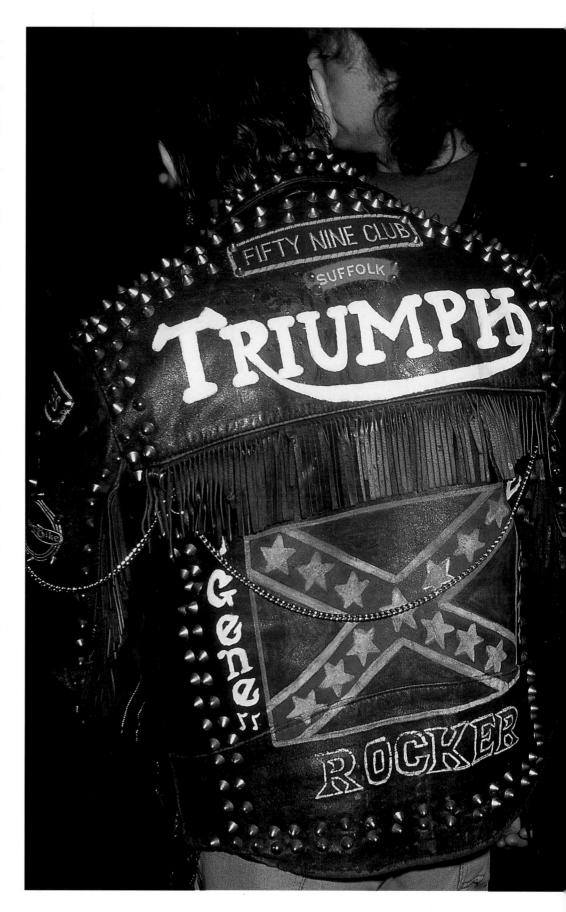

Left: *The 1958 T110 Tiger 650, a firm favorite with the ton-up crowd and the last stage before the definitive Bonneville. The engine's alloy 'Delta' cylinder head, which had been fitted since 1956, was modified for '58 to counter cracking.*

but in practice this seemed to have little ill effect.

That year too saw the introduction of the mainly export TR6 Trophy (or TR6/A Trophybird as it was known in its US West Coast incarnation), which took over as the Number 1 model in America. It was essentially a T110 adapted to be convertible for on/off road riding with touches like a smaller 3¼ gallon tank, which Europeans thought was just American taste, but which in fact also allowed a greater steering lock off-road. Instantly successful, TR6s would take the first twelve places in 1957's Big Bear Run enduro. 1956 was also the year when a twin carb head T110-engined machine in a streamliner shell took the two-wheeled World Speed Record at 214.4mph, on Bonneville salt flats, Utah. Though disputed

Below: *The Triumph 8 inch single leading shoe front brake was undergunned for a ton-plus motorcycle. Wheel rims were still 19 inch, front and rear.*

on a technicality, this was a great coup which would provide the name for the most famous twin of them all.

1957 saw the T110 restyled along with the rest of the range, with new 'mouth-organ' grille tank badges, which together with a chrome strip, separated the colors of two-tone schemes, another styling touch which Turner would carry off better than his imitators; on Triumphs they were also picked up by mudguards in one color, with a lined center stripe in the other. The T110's stock color however was now silver gray, though there was a blue and white two-tone option. 1958 was the T110's climax. With irresistible demand from the States, particularly after the optional twin carb T100 produced for 1957, the sports 650 was now also offered with an optional twin carb version of the Delta cylinder head. Unfortunately, on both this and the single carb head, an attempt was made to cure the cracking by reducing the size of the combustion chamber, but with inlet and exhaust valves with smaller diameter heads to suit, they did not run quite as fast as their predecessors.

However, this was the year when Texan Bill Johnson would take a twin carb T110 to 147.32mph at Bonneville and a new USA Class C (stock 650) national record. And at Thruxton in the new format 500 Mile production race, a twin carb T110 piloted by Dan Shorey and the young Mike Hailwood finally broke the Gold Star domination, coming home after an epic struggle just ahead of the ferocious Bob McIntyre on the 700cc Royal Enfield twin. It was a great exit for the 'ton-ten', because after that came the T120 Bonneville, and Triumph's previous 650 star would be relegated to second class citizenship.

The big Royal Enfield was a wild card from an independent factory. In many details their twins differed from the others, starting with their striking 692cc capacity, first seen on the touring Meteor in 1953, at a time when only BSA and Triumph had reached even 650. Royal Enfield's off-road

Left: *Triumph's pre-unit twins with their separate gearboxes, like the 1958 T110, had a class which their 1963-on unit successors could never quite match. Their handling may have been flawed, but the style is beyond reproach.*

competition successes with the robust 350 Bullet single were encouraging, especially as the big twin design was clearly dimensionally a doubled-up Bullet, even to the extent that its iron cylinders and alloy heads were separate castings. The oil compartment, like the Bullet's, was uniquely positioned, in the base and rear of the crankcase, from which the oil filter neck protruded. Although this arrangement avoided external oil lines, and included an effective cylindrical filter, the location of the oil within the cases, plus a mere 4 pint capacity, would mean severe overheating problems. And the separate cylinders, while well cooled and easy to work on, meant a lack of rigidity in an

Right: *Curvaceous chrome grilles of the T110's horn and tank badges evoked Cadillacs and Wurlitzer juke-boxes.*
Below: *The T110 may not have been the smoothest of Triumph's twins, but owners loved this Tiger's snarl, raw edges and speed.*

engine which, with its bolted-up gearbox, was also a stressed member of the open diamond, short wheelbase, Bullet-type frame. This caused 'shuffling' of the crankcase mouths, distortion, and the engine sometimes actually working loose in the frame. Before that they were the oil leaks which, exacerbated by the Royal Enfield's inadequate breathing system, were proverbial to the marque they called 'Royal Oilfield'.

Yet when running well the twin's engine was delightful, quick yet beefy, responsive, and quite smooth up to 90mph, with its tough one-piece crankshaft being balanced both statically and dynamically. In fact the 700 twin was full of contradictions. The impressive engine was let down by the crude Albion gearbox. Yet with magneto ignition and an alternator for lights, the Meteor's successor, the 40bhp Super Meteor with an all-welded frame was a good, solid machine, handsome in a chunky way, easy to work on, and with a wealth of thoughtful rider

Above: *The Royal Enfield 700 Constellation was a credible contender in the battle of the twins for a while. This Connie for 1961 demonstrates the model's compactness, as well as its lashings of chrome.*

features; to help remove the q.d. rear wheel, for instance, you could simply loosen the Armstrong rear suspension units' upper bolts, pull out two snap connectors, and remove the entire rear mudguard and seat assembly.

The Super Meteor was the bike favored by Syd Lawton, a highly talented development engineer and dealer who sponsored Bob McIntyre in the Thruxton 500 race. But in 1958, the year when 'Bob Mac' was aced by Mike Hailwood, Royal Enfield had introduced to the UK a new version of the 700 twin, the 405lb Constellation. The engine fitted new crankcases, with internal alterations including higher mounting for their racer-type cams, a stronger crankshaft, Nimonic valves already developed by Syd Lawton from BSA ones cut down to suit and with Gold Star alloy valve caps and collets. The Constellation breathed through a 1³/₁₆ inch Amal TT9 racing carburetor. A charismatic model with a big chrome and polychromatic red 4¹/₄ gallon petrol tank, chromed mudguards, a siamezed exhaust system and a claimed output for these early versions of 51bhp at 6,250rpm, it initially impressed when it was tested at 112mph. The only stylistic niggle among the café crowd was that Enfield's stubby version of Triumph's headlamp nacelle, dubbed the 'casquette', prevented the fitting of clip-on handlebars, so the Connie was limited to dropped 'ace' bars.

All too soon the model also developed a reputation for unreliability at prolonged high speeds, partly thanks to the fierce vibration at speeds over 90mph. Lawton's continuing struggle in the Thruxton 500 highlighted this. In 1958 the big Enfield had fallen behind due to a misfire and a split petrol tank (as had happened to Lawton's entry in '57). In 1959, hard-riding McIntyre had clutch problems and then dropped the bike on a chicane. In '60 the clutch cable broke, a fragment locked up the engine and had him off again. And in '61, the Enfield threw a con rod. On the street too the Constellation was dogged with problems from its tricky 'scissors-action' clutch which suffered from vibration and quickly ran out of clearance in traffic, as well as blown head gaskets, bad oil leaks, difficult starting and gearchanging. Royal Enfield had also failed to listen to Lawton, who knew already that the siamezed exhaust actually slowed the big twin's acceleration, and that a single Monobloc carb gave performance for them superior to the temperamental TT instrument. The production Constellation changed to twin Monoblocs during 1959, and to a conventional clutch for 1961, but by then, although the big Enfields continued to have their fans, the moment had passed. Excellent later 750 twins followed, the '63-on Interceptor, and particularly the completely redesigned 1969 Interceptor Series II, but the company was already done for and only just over a thousand of the latter were produced before the end came in the following year.

Back in the Fifties, another contender in the burgeoning big twin battle was the one from AJS/Matchless, heart of the Plumstead-based AMC group in south-east London, which had taken over Norton in 1952. As mentioned, their rear-springing had been a limiting factor but for 1957 this was redesigned to fit state-of-the-art 3-position Girling units, albeit with their own unique clevis-type bottom mounting until 1963. Thus equipped, the 500 twin, an excellently built tourer though vibratory at high revs, was bored out to 592cc. Why not to 650? Because the engine's design, like the Royal Enfield's, had featured separate iron cylinders and alloy heads. This meant that the cylinder center lines were a set distance apart, which imposed a limit on cylinder boring. It also meant that designing a twin carb cylinder head would be tricky. The design had further featured a unique center main bearing for the one-piece crankshaft, housed in a divider plate sandwiched between the two crankcase halves. This had been intended to keep vibration down, but some felt that it had the opposite effect, possibly because it inhibited crankshaft flexing which could itself deal with some of the shakes;

Above right: *1961's R.E. Constellation retained a siamezed exhaust but had changed its TT9 carb for twin Amal Monoblocs.*
Below right: *A handsome motorcycle, Royal Enfield's Constellation was a potentially excellent motor let down by its unreliability.*

Above: *Royal Enfield's 700 twin being hurled round Thruxton's lumpy airfield circuit by hard-charging Bob McIntyre. Despite 'Bob Mac's' guts and tuner Syd Lawton's skill, success eluded them when it counted most. Note the racer's twin pipe exhaust system.*

while others wondered if the bearing itself was rigidly enough located, by its six ¼ inch anchor studs, to damp down the vibes.

The 592cc version in AJS Model 30 or Matchless G11 form (virtually identical bar their badges) had been designed specifically to withstand high revs. The model ran from just 1956 to 1958, and in the latter year only, probably the best of all these twins was produced. This was the 600CSR, which sprang from the very similar export 600CS. The CS could well have stood for 'Convertible Scrambler', while CSR was held by the fast lads to signify 'Coffee Shop Racer'.

The US-oriented dual-purpose CS

featured the frame of the big single scrambler with its improved ground clearance, modified around the crankcase fixing points to take the twin engine. It fitted siamezed exhausts and polished alloy mudguards, a quickly detachable headlamp, a 2 gallon tank, a 21 inch front wheel with off-road tires and 7 inch full width hub brakes, plus a short dualseat covered in Vynide 'pig-skin'. Compression was 8.5:1 on the 32bhp twin, and ignition by Lucas magneto, which was gear-driven, like the engine's twin camshafts. The CSR simply substituted the standard roadster 3¾ gallon tank with its chrome plated side panels, low-level handle-

Left: *Matchless of Plumstead, London, was an historic name. Co-founder Charlie Collier had won the first Isle of Man TT on one in 1907.*
Right: *1958 Matchless G11CSR 600 twin. Note the unique 'clevis' bottom mountings for the Girling units introduced for 1957.*

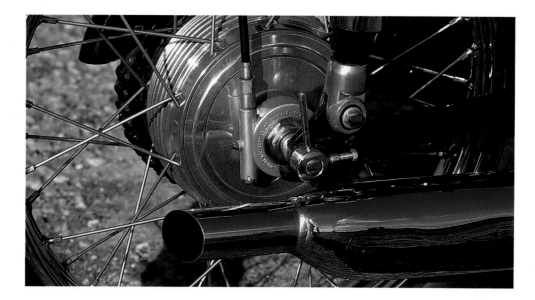

optional gearbox sprocket with an extra tooth, to help prevent over-revving. Willoughby then rode the bike back to London. Handling from the single down-tube frame and Teledraulic forks had not been the tautest due to comfortable springing, but no disgrace, and from then on the 600, with AMC's well known standard of finish, became a model to look out for, but more for the all-round Clubman rider than the ton-up crowd.

The lads went for the following year's 650CSR variant, the capacity achieved by a

Above: *The G11's slash-cut muffler was one of AMC's stylish touches. The rear wheel was easily removable thanks to its spindle Tommy bar. Full width hubs came in 1954.*

bars and a 19 inch front wheel plus road tires. Its four-speed AMC gearbox, recently also adopted on Nortons, was the best in the business, and the AJS/Matchless engines were notably free-revving, with a deep, 'ripping calico' exhaust note.

The 600 Sports Twin in Matchless G11CSR form caught the public's attention when in spring 1958, hard-riding journalist

Vic Willoughby rode one from London to MIRA, the motor industry's research track in Staffordshire, and waiting until lunchtime when the track was clear, reeled off a timed 102.926 miles round the track from a standing start in a single hour. The only variation from standard on the bike had been an

Right: *The G11's siamezed exhaust, 'Teledraulic' fork and flamboyant Vynide 'pig-skin' twinseat marked it out from the crowd.*
Below: *With a competition-bred frame, the 1958 G11CSR's handling was dependable, though the front brake was barely adequate.*

longer-throw crankshaft. But tank-splitting vibration was back in a big way, and early versions of the new crank suffered breakages at high speed before a different grade of nodular iron was used for it, though some reckoned the breakages also related to the adoption of electrics by crankshaft-mounted alternator for the cooking model twins from 1959. These CSR 650s did have a following, and for 1960 finally came with twin carbs and a redesigned head giving useful extra power, as well as superior handling from a heavier duplex-downtube frame. That year

saw a 650 AJS CSR variant win the Thruxton 500. But unreliability, some ill-judged American-inspired restyling and a deteriorating company situation, limited both production and development. An attempt to take the 650 out to 750 was aborted after only some 200 had been built, and the 750 Norton Atlas then powered a number of AMC-framed hybrid models, which lingered only a year or so after AMC went bust in 1966 and the old names passed to Norton–Villiers.

In one way this was just the tale of yet

another sound enough 500 twin roadster being taken out beyond its natural design parameters. Which is perhaps why the 1950-on BSA pre-unit twins began with an advantage; the Bert Hopwood-designed base model A10 was a 650, with the 497cc A7 virtually the same engine with a reduced bore and shorter stroke. There had been a long-stroke semi-unit 495cc A7 before that, and its sports version, the 1949 Star Twin, would be the only BSA pre-unit twin that was offered with twin carburetors as standard. BSA's philosophy, understandable in an era when one in

three large motorcycles pulled a sidecar, was to offer solid, workmanlike conveyances; and Hopwood's thinking on road bikes always favored good practical mid-range torque rather than marginally improved top speeds. He arrived at Small Heath from Norton in time to totally revise BSA's existing twins and to produce the 650 to match Triumph's Thunderbird. And the resulting A10 Golden Flash would be probably the toughest and most practical twin of them all.

Initially it was the plunger-framed A7 500 Star Twin sports model which led the way. With a single carb again and an all-iron engine, a trio of A7s fresh off the line won

Left: *The BSA twin's oil tank held 5 1/2 pints. Its screw-on cap was, usefully, a duplicate of the inspection cap in its primary chaincase.*
Below: *The alloy-head A7SS Shooting Star, a splendid 500 twin, with dark green chassis offsetting its polychromatic green paintwork.*

the Maudes Trophy in 1952 for a trouble-free 5,000 mile European trip which had included competing and taking Gold Medals in that year's ISDT. Though the experimental all-alloy versions may not have been a success, the same year in the USA, an A7 took the AMA Class C (standard 500) record at 123.69mph. And as mentioned, a brace of A7s won at Daytona in 1954. That year saw the sports 500 roadsters, for export only at first, adopting a version of the Gold Star's all-welded swinging-arm frame, which allowed a completely separate gearbox, and changing their name to the A7SS Shooting Star. These models came in a subtly handsome color scheme already initiated in 1953, with the cycle parts in dark green setting off the light polychromatic green mudguards, oil tank, tool box, and chrome-sided 4 gallon petrol tank with its unique large diameter black Star badge. With an alloy head and high-lift cams, the 32bhp BSAs, tested at 92 mph, outhandled their Tiger 100 rivals, but were nearly 25lb heavier, at 408lb dry. They were well liked as "easily the sweetest twin on the market", one seasoned journalist remembered, and Titch Allen added "exceptionally flexible and responsive in mid-range," with realistic top speeds not much down on the swinging-arm iron A10's 96mph.

The Shooting Star's green finish, a color previously traditional to BSA, was symbolically replaced by an optional bright red on the first sports 650 twin, the A10 Road Rocket, and this color would be synonymous with sports BSAs from then on. Introduced for export only in 1955, the A10RR also now fitted an alloy cylinder head as well as raised gearing, 8:1 compression and a TT9 carburetor. It was tested at 108mph, but also maintained the Golden Flash's reputation for ruggedness and a relatively long engine life, the only point to watch being its plain bush drive side main bearing. Handsome looking with chromed mudguards and a separate headlamp shell,

Right: *The handling on BSA's 1954-on swinging-arm frame with duplex front downtubes was second only to Norton's Featherbed among the twins of the Fifties. The 1955 A7SS also looked magnificent – another great all-rounder perhaps appreciated by Clubmen more than rockers.*

the café crowd also twigged early on that its looks and performance could be further racerized by adding Gold Star controls and gearbox internals.

Punishment in American competition was probably what led to the 1958 introduction for the BSA 650s of a new, strengthened, one-piece crankshaft, together with cylinder barrels with thicker base flanges, and the plain timing side main bearing changed from a white metal bush to a steel-backed lead-bronze one. These thick-flange engines were the ones to tune, but the sports 650, now known as the A10SR Super Rocket, took a step backwards stylistically, as it used the stock A10's unattractive headlamp cowling, though its chromed guards were now sports ones. On the plus side, the TT9 carburetor was replaced by a less fussy Monobloc, a slightly more efficient 4-spring clutch replaced the troublesome 6-spring one for 1960, and the 43bhp Super Rocket was good for 112mph.

The final act came in 1962–63 with the A10 RGS, for Rocket Gold Star. Already Gold Star specialist Eddie Dow had supplied some twenty customers with Super Rockets done up with clip-ons, rear-sets, close ratio gearboxes, Gold Star petrol tanks, etc. Belatedly the factory now followed suit, though the A10 was already under death sentence from its uncharismatic 1962 unit construction A65 successor. The Rocket Goldie was a beautiful machine, with siamezed exhausts and usually a Goldie silencer, chromed sports mudguards, separate headlamp, Gold Star fork legs allowing the use of the 190mm brake, a variant of the Gold Star frame, and bench-tested Super Rocket engines with a larger exhaust valve and 9:1 compression. The RRT2 gearbox was an option. Weighing in at around 395lb, the 46bhp Rocket Goldies came in Clubmans or Touring trim, and were produced for just 18 months. They were and remain a highly desirable swan-song for a tough, well-liked motorcycle.

Left: *BSA's leading sportster for 1961 was this 650 A10 Super Rocket. Its styling lacked the lightness of previous models, with the standard roadsters' tubular headlamp cowling, fully valenced mudguards and Triumph-style full-width hubs with 8 inch front brake.*

It should be borne in mind that while the sports A10s were relatively reliable, like all the other roadburners of the day they were maintenance intensive. Journalist Dave Minton who rode with a 90mph-plus crowd in this era, has calculated that for every hard day's riding on his '62 Super Rocket, he had to spend another day fettling it. In Dave's crowd, two machines stood out as able to take the pace reliably. One was a dustbin-faired A10, and the other a Velocette Venom Clubman single, "which while unable to overtake the rasping twins, was impossible to leave behind." Indeed, if there was a single cylinder equivalent of the durable pre-unit BSA twins, it was not the Gold Star, but the 500 Venom and 350 Viper. Velocette

Left: *Space-age decals and Royal Red paint job were easy ways of indicating the alloy head Super Rocket's sports character.*
Below: *The reliable A10 650 twin powerplant, producing 43bhp in Super Rocket form. A drip-tray under the carb protected the magneto.*

would be the last exponent of the Great British sporting single. In its way, this was as unlikely as the flight of the bumble bee.

A small family firm with great integrity, Velocette with their overhead cam K-series racing singles had been major innovators, pre-war. But post-war most of their resources had gone into an 'Everyman' fully enclosed light motorcycle, the L.E. Though this did not prove the major commercial success that was needed, luckily they had still retained the worthy and well-crafted MAC

350 ohv touring single. The high-camshaft 350 had been housed for 1953 in a rear-sprung frame meticulously crafted in Reynolds 531 and derived from the racers, and though you could flex its swinging-arm by hand, it provided hairline steering, probably the best of any British sprung-frame single. 1954 saw the MAC joined by the all-alloy MSS 500, with square (86 x 86mm) engine dimensions which while theoretically ideal, had in fact come about because, as the designer admitted, "we shortened its stroke

until it would fit" the existing MAC's spring-frame.

Velocette's West Coast American importer encouraged a not very satisfactory scrambles version of the 500 for dirt-track sport, and once again US tuning work on an engine got passed back to England and taken up by enthusiast dealers, who got the model involved in production endurance racing, and persuaded the factory to build a supersports version for 1956. This was the 500 Venom, together with a scaled-down

(72 x 86mm) 350 version, the Viper. Velocette quality and strength meant that as well as excellent handling, these were among the few machines of the day that could sustain really fast cruising speeds. The point

Right: *A10 Rocket Gold Star in Clubmans trim had a riding position as uncompromising as the Gold Star single – but it was easier to start.*
Below: *For many, the 1963 A10RGS Rocket Gold Star 650, with Super Rocket engine, was the ultimate BSA twin.*

was to be pushed home in 1961, when on the rough-surfaced track at Montlhéry in France, a team of English and French riders mounted on a Venom achieved a 12 hour World Record by averaging 104.66mph for that time, and a 24 hour record at an average speed of 100.05mph, which for 500cc machines still stands.

On the road, one downside was price – the Venom cost as much as a T110 650 twin – as well as looks that were already antiquated, a leak-prone primary chaincase, difficult starting, dubiously efficient belt-driven lighting, relatively heavy weight at 380lb dry, and a unique and uniquely complicated 16-spring

Left: *Velocette's rear suspension was as unorthodox as much of their design, with 'arcuate' sliding adjustment for the rear units.*
Below: *1961 Velocette Venom sports 500 single in Veeline variant, with a 'dolphin' fairing which aided mpg as well as fast cruising.*

clutch mounted inboard of the primary drive and providing minimal clearance, though it was pleasant enough when well set up. If you could live with all that, the big Velocettes delivered the goods like the thoroughbreds they were, and there would be a final development of them in the following decade.

But the fast machine most young riders had their eyes on was the 650 Triumph twin, and late in 1958 all the development strands came together in one archetypal model, the twin carb T120 Bonneville. As far back as 1955 a twin carb 650 had been tried out in hard use by scrambler Ken Heanes, and with the '57 twin carb T100, pressure from America for a production 650 to that specification became well-nigh irresistible. But it was resisted, by the ever-cautious Edward Turner. One reason may have been that he was in the process of turning over all the twin engines to unit construction, having begun in 1957 with the 350cc Twenty One, and may have wished to sugar the pill on the 650s by coinciding a unit version with the first twin carbs. He also, to his credit, distrusted the roughness that was creeping in on his engines with these performance hikes.

He was persuaded, however, and late in 1958, too late for inclusion in the catalog, the T120 was announced. Sporting twin Amal 1^{1}/$_{16}$ inch chopped Monoblocs with remote float mixing bowl, on its Delta-derived alloy head, the supersportster featured E3134 inlet and E3325 exhaust camshafts, the best all-round mix, plus 8.5:1 compression. All this increased output by 4 bhp over the T110, to 46bhp at 6,500rpm. Just as well, then, that the Bonneville also brought the introduction of a new one-piece crankshaft for all the 650s, with a pressed-in cast iron flywheel. Acceleration was intense, with 50 in 1st, 70 in 2nd, 88 in 3rd, and a top speed of 108mph, which could be hoisted to 115mph when it was racerized; but this performance was achieved, with the clever mix of cams, without loss of tractability, so that top gear had a range of 80mph.

Above right: *Velocette of Hall Green, Birmingham. The dent-prone alloy strips on these new-for-1961 tanks were unpopular.*
Below right: *Bruce Main-Smith pushes out the 1961 Venom Veeline Clubman which would lap Montlhéry for 24 hours at 100.05mph.*

The Bonnie was easy to start and easy to ride, and an instant, major hit commercially; Triumph had got it right. A quarter of a million T120 Bonneville's would be produced until 1972, which was nearly double the total of all the twins built post-war by their nearest rivals, BSA.

The Americans, at whom in some terms it had been aimed, were initially unhappy with the first Bonnie's styling. Not just the, ah, unusual Bright Tangerine and Gray two-tone color scheme, but also the fact that, while they had been hoping for a twin carb TR6, the early T120 retained the 4 gallon tank, the headlamp nacelle, plain fork shrouds, full mudguards, two level touring seat and pullback handlebars, where they wanted the TR6's small tank and fenders, separate chromed headlamp, etc, plus a tacho. "The T120 was the fastest but didn't look it!" as one observed. Their faith in Turner's judgement had already been undermined by the 'bath-tub' rear enclosure paneling he had imposed on the new 350 Twenty One, and that year, on the new unit

500, the lackluster poor-handling T100A.

For 1960 the Bonnie's color scheme was changed to a more characteristically Triumph Azure Blue and Pearl Gray, and it came with a separate chromed headlamp, independently mounted speedo, gaitered forks, sports mudguards and a low-level twinseat giving a somewhat 'jockey-like' riding position. The true Bonnie was emerging out of the chrysalis of the Fifties.

More substantial changes for 1960 had also seen Triumph looking at their handling problem. As well as redesigned, better-damped forks, the frame became a duplex downtube one with a steeper steering head angle. It was still of brazed-lug construction, though, still with a bolted-on sub-frame, and the swinging-arm was still unbraced. It provided slightly heavier steering, and had to be put into corners more deliberately, but while the bike was still highly maneuverable and a class leader for lightness at 390lb dry, the front end now felt reassuringly less light at speed. This 650 also vibrated less than its predecessors. Though a magneto was retained,

lighting now came from an RM15 alternator.

But in America as Edward Turner watched the 1960 Big Bear Run, a rider suffered a fatal accident when, under the pressure of competition, the downtubes of his new frame fractured beneath the steering head lug. The frame's unreliability had already caused many US warranty claims – as had the alternator ("beyond bad," recalled one American dealer, and a Lucas rep had been booed at a 1961 dealer convention). So for 1962 a strengthening tube in the form of a lower tank rail was added to the 650's frame. This cured the breakages, but unfortunately transmitted much more vibration, not too badly for the rider but enough to provoke an epidemic of broken petrol tank straps, and cause worse frothing of the carbs' remote float chamber, so from that year the instruments became standard Monoblocs. The steering head angle became a couple of degrees less steep, to suit US cross-country competition; the Bonnie got a fatter rear tire, 3 gallon petrol tank, and magneto with automatic advance, all to the same end.

The smaller tank completed the elegant aura of these hot twins, creating a paradox which one owner summed up as follows: "They're very dainty, really – but all the butch berks wanted one!" Which helped make the reet petite Bonneville the most stolen machine of its generation. And the best loved. Many feel that these pre-unit 650s were the ultimate class act among parallel twins.

More American influence could be discerned in 1962, when that year's Bonnie fitted a heavier flywheel with the greater inertia more suitable off-road, though the tuned 650's were already known for excellent low-down grunt. Then it was time for another major change. But the increasing Stateside input of the previous couple of years was partly due to an ominous development. The bottom had dropped out of the home motor-

Below: *In classic Triumph Sky Blue and Silver colors, this 1961 T120 Bonneville represented a near-final flowering of the pre-unit sports twins. Its uncharacteristic duplex front downtube, strengthened for that year, can be clearly seen.*

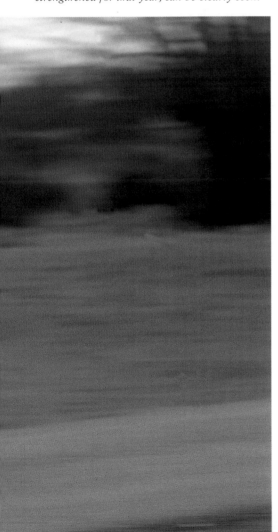

cycle market. The restitution of savage h.p. restrictions once the 1959 election had been won; an anti-rocker Press campaign resulting in the 1961 Hughes–Hallett Bill restricting learner riders to 250cc machines; and above all, increasing affluence plus the advent of affordable cars, exemplified by the Mini, was killing off the base ride-to-work market.

In addition, with the opening of the first M1 motorway late in 1959, and the abandonment of previous Tory pro-Rail policies, Britain's road system began dragging itself into the late twentieth century; existing British motorcycles, largely tailored to roads based on winding cart tracks, were not best suited to this brave new world, and people were realiz-

Above: *The T120 Bonneville's twin splayed Amal 376 Monobloc carburetors were the ultimate go-faster badge in its day.*

ing it. In the awful three year yawp before the Sixties really got going, the industry suffered a frightening slump; sales in 1961 were down 35 per cent on the previous twelve months. Under the circumstances it was 'God Bless America!' and the export market which Triumph above all others had helped develop there. And it was the end of an era.

Below: *The Bonnie's separate, chromed head - lamp shell (still housing the practical ammeter) was a much appreciated styling touch.*

1961 Triumph T120 Bonneville

This 1961 Sky Blue and Silver pre-unit twin carb 650, the T120 Bonneville, was for many the pinnacle of Triumph twins for looks and overall charisma. Its frame had been strengthened that year with an additional lower tank rail, which halted previous fractures – but unfortunately transmitted more vibration. With reliable magneto ignition and excellent build quality due to Triumph boss Edward Turner's policy of restricting output to encourage demand, today these '58–62 pre-unit Bonnies fetch the highest prices of any Triumph twin.

Specification

Model
Triumph T120 Bonneville
Year
1961
Bore and stroke
71 x 82mm
Displacement
649cc (39.58cu. in.)
Bhp
46bhp @ 6,500rpm
Top speed
108mph (174kph)
Fuel consumption (overall)
64mpg
Transmission
4-speed
Wheelbase
55in.
Wheel and tire dimensions
3.25 x 19in (front); 4.00 x 18in (rear)
Frame type
Duplex downtube cradle
Weight (dry)
393lb (178kg)

1963–1969

"TWILIGHT OF THE GODS"

MOTORCYCLING IN BRITAIN started the Sixties with a bad name, with public holiday seaside clashes between rockers and scooter-riding Mods, though these were often orchestrated, encouraged and then exaggerated by the media, and look mostly like youthful high spirits beside the emerging viciousness of the hard-core biker gangs in America.

Meanwhile, there was more traffic, more motorways, sodium road lighting, traffic wardens, MOT tests and the first overall 70mph speed limit in 1966, with compulsory helmets to follow in 1971. Slowly the British industry responded to the changing times with, by the late Sixties, tires from Avon and Dunlop which performed better in the rain

Left: Norton 'short' Roadholder front forks and 8 inch single leading shoe front brake were both the best in the business.
Below: 650 Norton engine in SS form, with twin Amal 376 Monobloc carburetors mounted at a steep downdraft angle.

and at high speed. These were complemented by new road surfaces with better grip. Though brakes improved, motorcycles however, unlike cars, did not get disc brakes yet, apparently because that would have meant redesigning front forks. Direction indicators from Lucas too were delayed until 1971, and not reliable when they arrived, but the mid-Sixties had at least seen the changeover from 6 to 12 volt electrical systems, allowing more effective lights.

There was one moderate success story

among the UK motorcycle slump of the early Sixties. The Norton twin reached its peak sports form in the shape of the 650SS. Bert Hopwood had quit BSA when Edward Turner gained ascendancy there, and returned to Norton as Managing Director, taking with him his talented cohort, Doug Hele. With Hopwood ready to enlarge the Norton twin from 600 to 650cc, it was Hele who improved the original cylinder head with its rather narrow port centers to the single carburetor inlet manifold. He settled on 20° downdraft inlet ports for a new head with wider centers, ready for twin carburetors; he also widened its exhaust angle in plain view, enabling the exhaust ports to be shortened and thereby collect less heat.

The head was introduced for 1960 in single carb form, together with larger inlet valves. This was the year that saw a new version of the Featherbed frame, the 'Slimline'. Ostensibly this was introduced to improve rider comfort, by narrowing the previously parallel top tubes at the seat nose, allowing a

narrower nosed seat and slimmer tank. However, factory sources have said that the real reason was so that the bigger twins could fit a version of the enclosure body paneling, which, in an unfortunate imitation of Edward Turner's 350 Twenty One, Hopwood had fitted to his unit 1959 250 Jubilee light twin. This was duly done, but luckily not on the flagship 650SS. The 'Slimline' was said by some to cause a slight reduction in handling virtuosity, but if so it was only at racing speeds. The larger engined machine, after being introduced for 1961 as an export-only model, the 650 Manxman, came on the home market for 1962.

By the time that happened, all the twins could be had in SS form, with the new alloy cylinder head in downdraft, twin carburetor form, with parallel inlet tracts; this also replaced a previous twin carb head with splayed inlet ports developed for the 600 'desert sled' N15 Nomad, which had been available as an option for the 500 and 600 since mid-1958. The new head was coupled

Above: *No chrome for the headlamp shell on restrained Norton. The famous 'straight' handlebars derived from the Vincents.*
Right: *Handsome, poised and compact, the 1964 Norton 650SS. The twins had switched to 'Slimline' Featherbed frames for 1960.*

with a Daytona camshaft and flat-based cam followers, two rate valve springs, hollow barrel-shaped light alloy pushrods, opened-up, polished ports, and for the 650, a compression of nearly 9:1. There were single carb Standard and paneled De Luxe 650s, but the 650SS turned its back on the alternator electrics adopted by most of the other twins for 1958. It reverted to the more reliable magneto for ignition, though it retained an alternator for lights; only toward the end of its production life, in mid-1967, would it change to full coil ignition. It was not only an alternator's relative fragility that made a mag desirable; some, including production race wizard Syd Lawton, believed that it was weight distribution from alternators hung on

Left: *This uncharismatic die-cast and chromed Norton badge went with the narrower tank on the 'Slimline' Featherbed frame. The tank held 3.62 gallons.*

smaller sportsters. This was really a great all-rounder, with dry weight just under 400lb.

All this was combined with Featherbed handling, which, as the author can testify, was so good that you forgot about it. This understated quality was mirrored by the 650SS's low, unostentatious stance and arrow-like straight lines, echoed everywhere, in the Slimline models' long spiked chrome tank badge, the Norton 'straight' handlebars, the horizontal silencers without the frivolity of tailpipes, and the rather austere finish in plain black and silver, the traditional Norton colors but unalleviated by tank lining or anything much else, though chromed mudguards, optional at first, soon became standard. Yet despite its low profile and late arrival, the 650SS was one of the great icons of the rocker age. Hair-line steering – "you can steer it with your nose," as one owner put it – and rock-steady handling were there, with an unfailing steadiness. The downside, the price of the above really, was a rather harsh quality to the ride, which could account for it inspiring more respect but less affection than the Triumphs. But the Bonnie was now equaled and surpassed, a point made by Thruxton 500 victories for the 650 'Lawton Norton' piloted by Brian Setchell, who was partnered on two occasions by Phil Read, for 1962, '63 and '64.

the end of the crankshaft, together with that of heavier clutches fitted to cope with rising power, which affected the handling of all British twins at this time. Lawton partially cured it by rebuilding his machines' wheels with their rims pulled fractionally to the left.

With a redesigned engine retaining the 600's bore but using a new, still stronger crankshaft with a wider flywheel, to take the previous 82mm stroke up to 89mm, the 650SS was a phenomenon – "approaches two miles a minute yet eats out of your hand," as one road test put it. For the tractability and low down torque that had been rather sacrificed on the previous tuned Norton twins was back in force, yet the motor punched out 49bhp at 6,800rpm, meaning 0–50mph in 6 seconds plus regular top speeds of 112mph with more available on occasions, and vibration less than on the

With the potent 650 Norton engine there was theoretically no longer any need for rockers to drop Triumph motors into race-kitted Featherbed frames to create the previous hybrid ultimate, the Triton. But in fact they still did, because not only was the 650SS still 10 per cent dearer than the top Triumph, but production was still limited by the frames being made at Reynolds (on the same jigs) – and by upheaval in the company. After run-ins with the AMC bosses, Hopwood had left in May 1961, and mismanagement plus the disastrous home mar-

Left: *Useful gear indicator on the excellent AMC/Norton 4-speed box. Norton twins would remain pre-unit to the end, avoiding unit engine's problems.*

ket meant that AMC closed Norton's old Bracebridge Street factory in Birmingham and early in 1963, moved production down to Plumstead in South-East London, which further disrupted output.

Before that, Doug Hele had crafted the 500cc Domiracer which came in a sensational 3rd in the 1961 Senior TT, with a best lap speed of 100.36mph, not to be bettered by a pushrod machine for another eight years. He had also taken the 650 twin out to 750, to satisfy an American demand for a roadster with enough grunt to go from 20 to 100mph in top gear. An export-only model from 1962 until 1964, the beefy 750 Atlas carried a vibration penalty, as Hele had warned it would, which made it impractical and painful to exploit its performance for long on tarmac. AJS/Matchless would however slot it into their brazed-lug frame, which soaked up some of the shakes, to

create some potent hybrid desert sleds, as well as roadsters with an identity crisis; and, as we shall see, it would then form the basis of the last great Norton twin.

Doug Hele left Norton in 1962 when the move south was announced and joined Hopwood back at Triumph, where the main task was preparing the unit construction version of the commercially all-conquering Bonneville. Turner was about to retire as Managing Director but his styling meant that the new Bonnie cleverly kept continuity with the old, the shape of its gearbox still being retained despite the unified

Below: *Triumph 650s like this 1968 T120 Bonneville had made the transition from pre-unit to unit construction relatively painlessly, with styling touches like the 'horizontal comma' flute cast into the primary chaincase. The frame reverted to a single downtube.*

construction. Hele and a fellow designer also fresh from Norton, Brian Jones, also contributed crucially, for it was they who finally tackled the Triumph's handling problem. The chassis returned to the characteristically Triumph single downtube design, but with the downtube in stronger $1^{5}/_{8}$ inch diameter tubing. And at the back end, the unsupported swinging-arm, now carried in a new brazed-in forged lug, was secured to the rear engine mounting plates. These in turn were bolted to struts on the rear sub-frame. The improvement in rear end stiffness was immediately noticeable, and from then on Triumph handling was increasingly a plus point. Through the decade Hele would be responsible for progressive uprating, with more stiffness, less front end lightness and tauter steering.

In the engine, there was a new light alloy head with increased finning that featured

better gas sealing between the cylinders, and a ninth, center-mounted cylinder stud which finally countered the previous cracking; the 'nine-stud head' was the one, from then on. With this head, the difference in valve timing between the single and twin carb heads had now gone, and from now on knowledgeable road riders would often prefer the TR6 Trophy which was virtually a single carb Bonnie, with only minute differences in top end performance, if any, and without the need for constant balancing of the two instruments. Both models were really light, with the Bonnie just 363lb, 30lb lighter than their lackluster BSA opponent, the unit A65.

Something, however, had been lost for Triumphs with the move to unit construction. Firstly, the ride experience was noticeably harsher. Factory man Hughie Hancox wrote that "the problems with the larger (unit) twins were all due to rigidity. The earlier pre-unit bikes did vibrate but it was liveable with due to the bike's overall flexibility. Having separate engine, gearbox and transmission, a lot more give – and indeed, forgiveness – was apparent, but with the unit construction 650s ... there was no forgiveness at all." Primary drive was now by stronger but less flexible duplex chain, and compression had risen to 8.5:1, and would go to 9:1 in 1966. Triumph countered with attention to footrests and engine mountings, but from now on if driven hard the Bonneville began to vibrate badly enough for bits to regularly fracture or drop off.

The other major new area of grief was the electrics. The magneto had gone – Lucas were phasing them out of production – and alternators for coil ignition with auto advance were cheaper. To buy, at any rate. For of all the faults that motorbikes are heir to, electrical ones are the most maddening, because they stop you rolling. And the Lucas 6 volt system fitted at this time was severely flawed. The 4CA contact breaker, driven by the exhaust camshaft, featured two sets of

Right: *1968 was one of the top years for the unit T120 Bonneville. The new two-way damped front fork and excellent twin leading shoe front brake, were complemented by an even stronger swinging-arm than the original improved version for 1963.*

Left: *Probably the best British production drum brake, the 1968 Triumph twin leading shoe stopper was given a safer cable run for 1969–70, with a bell-crank forward lever.*

center of gravity, which reduced, if not entirely cured, front end lightness at 100mph and over, plus its attendant high speed weave.

One area where the latter mod was not entirely appreciated was in American AMA National TT racing. This US sport was very different from the Isle of Man TT road racing from which it had originally derived its name. Typically it was run on dry clay, on a quarter mile kidney-shaped track giving both left and right turns, with an aviating high jump half way round, thus combining the most spectacular elements of dirt-track and scrambling. The AMA excluded any ohv bike larger than 500cc from the popular Class C dirt-track racing until 1969, but the TTs were still one area, along with desert racing, record breaking and the drag strip, where the 650 Bonneville could shine. In the Sixties, Triumph 40 cubic inch twins won more American TT races than all other makes combined.

Below: *The 'eyebrow' tank badge had replaced the 'mouth-organ' for 1966, and continued to define Triumph's two-tone paint schemes, which were the best.*

points required to fire the twin rubber-mounted ignition coils attached to the frame. But the two sets of points, mounted on one plate together with the condensers, could not be timed individually for each cylinder, and the timing had to be compensated for by varying the gap of the points. Which would only open precisely 180° apart if the camshaft rotated exactly centrally. Which it usually did not. Erratic sparks could lead to vibration and ultimately piston seizure. In addition voltage was regulated by 'switch control' i.e. turning on the lights, without which the battery overcharged and failed. And with coil ignition, unlike a magneto, if the battery failed, you had no sparks. 12 volt electrics with Zener diode voltage control for 1966, and independently adjustable 6CA points for 1968, would offer some cure, though the coils themselves would remain vulnerable to heat, and the switches to vibration. All this was one cause of warranty claims rising steeply throughout the decade.

Over the years Triumph pegged away at the 650's other problems, which included occasional failure of drive side main bearings, cured by the change for 1966 to a heavy duty single-lipped roller. The cycle

parts were steadily improved. 1964 brought better damped and stronger 'external spring' front forks. By 1966 race experience had brought a change in the steering head angle. This was reduced to 62°, by means of a new front frame with a shorter top tube; the effect of this was to lower the engine and the

The purpose-built tool for this achievement was a 1963 West Coast variant of the T120C 'Competition Sports' US export version of the Bonnie. With no lights, tachometer only, straight-through high level exhausts, plus 'ready-fix' racing number plate fixing points on the rear lifting handles and front headlamp brackets, though built at Meriden rather than in the US, this was one hot number. Initially compression was a sky-high 12:1, twin full-race camshafts were fitted, and 'chopped' Monobloc carbs with a flexibly mounted remote float bowl. Giving a claimed 52bhp, the model was an instant success on the tracks, a fact celebrated by it being designated the T120CTT 'TT Special' for 1964, and supplied to both coasts, though Californian tracks like Riverside and Ascot were its true metier.

1965 saw the compression ratio dropped to 11:1 and the TT Special adopt its most characteristic feature visually, new low-level 1³/4 inch diameter open exhaust pipes, which curved under the crankcase and stopped dead just behind the engine; claimed output rose to 54bhp. The open pipes supplied even better mid-range torque, which together with the well-balanced chassis (and an affordable price) made the TT Special so popular. The model fitted shortened rear units plus competition units in the front forks, and a 3.25 x 19 inch front with a 4.00 x 18 inch rear for the wheels and tires, at a time when stock T120s came with 18 inch wheels at both ends. It also featured batteryless Energy Transfer ignition, but that system's flaws did not affect 100 lap races with no re-start. A final sexy touch were the narrower 2¹/2 (US) gallon tanks fitted for 1966.

As mentioned, the Bonnie's '66 shift to a 62° head angle was not popular with the track racers, who favored the previous 65°

Below: *Fat anti-vibration handlebar grips and ball-ended control levers were standard on the 1968 Bonneville. A new 3-position toggle switch in the headlamp shell indicated the improved electrics. The ignition switch was repositioned on the left fork top side.*

angle, and many continued to compete on those chassis well into the Seventies, although by then specialist frames from Trackmaster and Sonicweld had come in to take on Harley's '70-on XR-750. With the T120CTT there was naturally a downside to pushing what was basically a production machine to the limit. Top tuner Danny Macias noted that "we broke a lot of crankshafts before I started Magnafluxing them between races." But as flamboyant ace Eddy Mulder confirmed, "The TT Special was a truly excellent TT bike right out of the box...It was a rocket." Discontinued after 1967, the TT Special became an enduring part of the Bonneville legend.

Bonnies were on a roll. UK production race successes had begun once Syd Lawton changed to Triumphs, with works legend Percy Tait plus Rod Gould winning the Thruxton 500 in 1967 followed by victory in the very first Isle of Man Production TT by John Hartle. By then there was also major input from Doug Hele's successful big race effort with the 500 at Daytona. But though

the Bonnie's bigger carburetors, plus patient work with valves, stronger valve springs, cam followers and camshafts (which both became the E3134 profile for 1967) hoisted power output to 48bhp, there was a penalty attached to this quest for performance. The stronger bearings for 1966 had been accompanied by the flywheel being lightened by 2½lb, and this led to vibration 'peaks' above 5,000rpm becoming more intense, with a consequent rash of warranty claims as this split the new, narrower petrol tanks. This would remain a problem until 1969, and was a symptom of a wider worry. Factory man John Nelson in his definitive model history *Bonnie* records that with the T120's ever-increasing state of tune "many in Meriden felt that they were transforming a high speed tourer into a disguised production racer".

That was one cause for concern, and the other arose from the Bonneville's success itself, and the sheer volume of production. Edward Turner had held this down to an optimum of around 25,000 motorcycles made at Meriden, with some 6,500 going to America. But when he stepped down in 1964, his BSA/Triumph group successor, the dynamic Harry Sturgeon, initiated a sales push which in view of the UK slump was entirely US-oriented. In the peak season of 1968–69, from a Triumph production total of 37,059 the booming American market took 25,407 – while the UK home market accounted for just 2,143. The labor force with strong unions could not help realizing the leverage which this gave them, with a company dependent on the American market's predominantly limited selling season – California and the West took 10,500 machines in 1967, but the East 18,200. Frequent unofficial industrial action disrupted an already stressed production process. The result was a paradox. From 1967 to 1970 the very best Bonnies of all were made, but with extreme variations in build quality. As Meriden churned out twins at a rate of up to 900 a week, engines and part-completed machines piled up in the

Left: *BSA A65LC Lightning Clubmans 650 twin, produced for 1965 only, featured a humped racing seat with the hallowed Gold Star badge on its rear.*

aisles, and bikes were shipped Stateside with parts missing. British bikes with their vibration, electrical unreliability, oil leaks (though usually these came after amateur rebuilds) became one of motorcycling's stock jokes. That did not stop demand for the Bonneville outstripping supply.

Yet 1968 was one of the best Bonneville years ever. Electrics, in conjunction with '67s less vulnerable resin-encapsulated alternator rotors, had the 6CA points, the Zener diode now with a heat sink and moved to a cooler position beneath the headlamp, the ignition switch finally moved from its previous unpopular under-seat location to the left hand fork cover, matching the toggle headlight switch on the headlamp shell.

The handling took another leap forward with a new race-bred swinging-arm, longer, and from mid-year, of thicker section tube, mounted on a new lug with heavier corner fillets for additional stiffness, which substantially improved high speed handling. The

front forks also came good, gaining true two-way damping, precisely controlled via a shuttle valve damper attached to the lower end of the stanchions. And between the forks was a new 8 inch twin-leading shoe brake which was finally up to the Triumph's ton-plus performance – it was, in fact, just about the best production drum brake the industry ever produced. This was true fruition and the '68 Bonnie looked the part, taut yet charismatically appealing, a real star.

BSA's unit twins, the A50 500 and the A65 650, by contrast had started in 1962 as the ugly sisters. The rounded lines of their motors' 'power-egg' styling was referred to as 'those water-melon engines' in the States,

Below: *Some Americans derided the 'power egg' shape of BSA's unit twin motor as 'water melon engines' but it showed well enough on this 1965 A65 Lightning Clubmans, with twin Monobloc carbs, siamezed exhaust, gold color scheme and cut-back side panels.*

while rocker Mike Clay in his book *Café Racers* confirms that "to the café crowd they looked hideous". Introduced as tourers, by the time the twin carb Lightning appeared in 1965, the short stroke engine with the triplex primary chain had a dire reputation for the worst vibration of all the parallel twins, plus all the alternator electrical troubles that God gave Triumph, and then some. In the BSA's case they centred round contact breakers causing problems for the ignition, with a 'rogue' spark, stemming from a mismatched contact breaker cam profile and spring tension, causing misfiring and ultimately piston seizure at speed, as the timing went haywire.

This was eventually sorted in 1966 by Pete Colman in America, but the BSA unit twin engines also suffered problems with the lipped roller timing side main bearing which had soon replaced their original drive side ball race. The lipped roller was prone to turn in its housing, loosen off and fragment its

ever Syd Lawton had found that for UK production racing, out of the Triumph, BSA and Norton 650s, the BSA was both the slowest and the worst handling. BSA attempted to reverse public perception of the model by hiring the great Mike Hailwood in 1965 to contest a prestigious, big-money production race, the first Hutchinson 100 at Silverstone.

Above: *A65LC twin at Brands Hatch in production race trim, with upswept exhaust and 'dolphin' fairing. But the BSA unit twins were outshone by Triumphs and Nortons, on the track and off.*

cage. This allowed the timing side plain bush to also turn in its housing and cut off the oil supply to the big ends. BSA discovered the solution to this during their unsuccessful race effort at Daytona in 1966 and '67. It took the form of substituting a roller bearing with a built-in ball race for the timing side main, in combination with an end-fed crankshaft conversion. But they failed to implement it on production machines. Troublesome clutches, and alloy oil pumps inadequate at high speed, were further problems.

A pity, because otherwise the engine had a lot going for it. While it could settle down as a steady performer at normal speeds, it was also potentially very fast, usefully faster than its pre-unit predecessors and also with strong mid-range power. Success in sidecar racing by BSA factory man and eight-times Champion Chris Vincent spoke for itself, and in America Dick Mann averred that by 1969 the A65 if fitted with stronger con rods was "a great racing engine". Earlier how-

Right: *The 1965-only A65LC Lightning Clubmans was one of the most handsome incarnations of BSA's unit twins. With tuned engine and close ratio gearbox, it had Go as well as Show. But the market for café racers was fading fast.*

In pouring rain Mike beat the Triumphs of Percy Tait and Phil Read, but then he could win on anything, and his works-provided A65's frame had been discreetly but distinctly non-standard, with an altered steering head angle.

1965's genuine production racer was the handsome twin carb A65 Lightning Clubmans, with siamezed exhausts, chromed fork shrouds and rear brake plate, a racing seat sporting a Gold Star badge on its rear hump, and the gold and chrome tank echoing the well-liked old A10 Golden Flash colors. But it was the Rocket Gold Star which the A65LC really sought to echo, with its rev counter, dropped 'ace' handlebars, rear-set footrests combined with a reversed gear selector camplate, and its close ratio gearbox. And as with the Rocket Goldies, each engine, with its big valves and high performance camshaft, was individually bench-tested. The result was a claimed 51bhp at 6,750rpm, in a highly charismatic package.

For 1966 it was followed by the ultra-

flamboyant A65S Spitfire Mk II (there had been no Mk I), with its big bright red fiberglass petrol tank and a pair of Amal GP racing carburetors. The chassis reached its most satisfactory form, redesigned with a 62° steering head angle and better damped forks. With stonking 10.5:1 compression, BSA claimed a sensational 55bhp for the model, and John Cooper won the 1966 Hutchinson 100 on one, but high speed vibration on the model was very severe. Following a *Motor Cycle* road test at MIRA which recorded a highest one-way speed of 123mph, making it the fastest production roadster of its day, BSA at least had a great

Right: *1966 A65S Spitfire Mk II sported alloy wheel rims, a Gold Star-derived 190mm brake, and forks with improved damping.*
Below: *The Spitfire Mk II's big selling points were its massively red 5 gallon fiberglass petrol tank, and twin Amal GP carburetors.*

slogan for the Spitfire – "120mph straight from the crate".

An American *Cycle World* road test correctly identified the Spitfire Mk II as exemplifying the trend in motorcycles away from basic transportation to sporting roadburners, no longer made for economy, but "made to *go* and to look and sound sporty". On the Spitfire Mk II the sports appearance was enhanced by alloy wheel rims, those twin GP carbs, the Gold Star's 190mm front brake though now in a full-width hub, and on the US models, a slick 2 (US) gallon fiberglass red and cream gas tank with a spiked, pear-shaped BSA badge decal.

But as *Cycle World* observed, weight-saving from the vulnerable alloy wheel rims was not significant – at a claimed 383lb dry, the Spitfire was just 9lb lighter than an A65 Lightning. The GP carbs lacked a throttle stop and thus idled poorly, while the distance from the needle jet to the spray nozzle

in the carburetor meant rather poor throttle response from low speeds, with the possibility of stalling if you overdid it. There were also mysterious flat spots, including a severe one at 6,000rpm, which the magazine attributed to the GPs' vibration-sensitive remote float chamber, but which in fact later proved to have been due to the 'rogue' spark. The 'legendary' 190mm brake, which in real money was less than 7½ inches in diameter though with a 2 inch wide shoe to compensate, proved not very powerful and squeaked badly. And the 2 gallon tank provided a range of less than 100 miles, and was criticized for it – ironically, at the time in the UK, BSA/Triumph were taking flak for impractical touches like that which were aimed at the US market, and then seasoned American riders did not appreciate them either!

The picture was not all black. *Cycle World* recognized how the A65's narrow valve angles meant that the 10.5:1 compression ratio could be achieved without recourse to a top-heavy, high crown piston. They also praised its reassuringly stable handling and good comfort. The sorting of the 'rogue' spark and other changes for 1967, including compression lowered to 10:1 and the carburetors changed to twin Amal Concentrics, seemed to have a good effect on vibration for the rider, and the Mk III Spitfire was actually quite tractable and relatively smooth. The same went for the final Mk IV in 1968, but the fact that it sported the excellent Triumph two-way damped front fork and twin leading shoe front brake, indicated where the real development was now being done within the BSA/Triumph group. 1969 changes to the twin's chassis were a retrograde step, with top-heaviness and increased vibration. The A65 never approached the Bonnie's popularity. Though flawed in detail and mis-styled, the final 1971–72 models in the group's new oil-bearing frame were fine motorcycles, but by then no 650 was at the cutting edge.

Right: *The 1966 A65S Spitfire Mk II was good-looking and charismatic, but compared to a Triumph equivalent its style was cobby and rather lumpy. Handling had improved, but vibration meant that the 54bhp performance could not be indulged in to the*

Above: *Velocette Thruxton's excellent 7¹/₂ inch twin leading shoe front brake. This 1969 example was the later type made by Tommy Blumfeld. Both kinds worked well.*

The same applied earlier and even more so for 500 singles, but there was at least one shining exception. Velocette's big one reached its apogee in 1965. It had been available in bits and pieces earlier, but the first full Thruxton Venom came on the market in June of that year. Its main component mechanically was a new cylinder head, which had evolved initially via a tuner used by the American importer, as well as from development by racing men in both South Africa and New Zealand. Among other things, the American tuner, Don Brown, dealt with a Velocette problem at racing speeds which had arisen from both the pushrods of the high camshaft engine being carried in a single large chromed pushrod tube. This dictated relatively long rocker arms, which in turn caused the danger of valves tangling at high engine speeds. This

Right: *The Velocette's superb, forgiving handling at speed was found perhaps at its best on their ultimate sportster, the Thruxton. Velocette, fast and dependable, engenders fierce marque loyalty to this day, and with the Thruxton it is easy to see why.*

had helped limit revs on the Venom to 6,200 rpm. So Brown reduced both the diameter of the exhaust valve, and the included angle between the valves. Only by a little, but it resulted in much better breathing, as there was now room for the size of the inlet valve to be increased; on the production Thruxton it would settle on a memorably large 2

inches. These valves were no longer at risk of tangling, and the engine could now be safely revved to 7,500rpm. The colonial racers then boosted performance further by giving the head a squish-band.

Fed by a 1½ inch GP carb on an extended finned inlet spacer, this head became available at the famous West London Velocette

dealers L. Stevens, along with a load of other desirable goodies. Combined on one machine, they were presented to the factory. Velocette's Bertie Goodman approved, and contributed an idea of his own. To save on crafting a new camshaft, yet achieve quicker valve opening and closing, the valve train was altered using shortened pushrods which were

now in one piece, and quick-lift cam followers of an increased radius. To help with the problem of the tapered roller main bearings pushing at and cracking the crankcases at high revs, Thruxton cases themselves were made heavier, and were heat-treated. The Thruxton produced 41bhp.

Black and gold finishes were temporarily

out of fashion, but the Thruxton presented itself in equally classic silver, but differentiated from that on Norton or BSA singles by gold tank lining and transfers, and subtly combined with very dark blue cycle parts and dualseat. The petrol tank was cut away to accommodate the GP carb, and the oil tank carried a perforated heat-shield. There was an excellent 7½ inch twin-leading shoe front brake, at first sourced from specialist John Tickle, with a later version for the factory made by Tommy Blumfield. Alloy wheel rims, a swept-back exhaust, clip-ons, rear-sets and their appropriate linkages, close-ratio gear sets and two-way damped fork internals, added up to a complete factory café racer, and an extremely handsome one. Thruxtons did well in production racing, regularly winning the 500 class of, appropriately, the Thruxton 500, even though the race was by then run elsewhere.

There were few drawbacks. When the rear-sets' linkages became worn, the gear

Left: *Its subtle dark blue and silver finish set the Thruxton's lines off well. The fishtail silencer was still needed for best performance.*
Below: *With no more magnetos, late Velos like this 1969 Thruxton adopted coil ignition, but kept the forward-mounted belt-driven dynamo.*

lever would foul the exhaust pipe and make changes, particularly downshifting, hard; and the GP carb as usual lacked tickover. Performance was on a par with the 500 Gold Stars, with best speeds of up to 115mph. Yet the Velocette was a far more civilized ride, with the narrow crankcases and main bearings set close to the steel flywheels providing a remarkably smooth ride at all speeds. Starting the 9:1 compression Thruxton might be even more of knack than with a cooking Velo, but the strong engine and gearbox plus the excellent front brake meant that prolonged 90mph cruising was both possible and realistic, and the motor also accelerated steadily and well from 4,000 rpm. With a shift to coil ignition in mid-1968, the Thruxton was made right up until the factory, the last of the independents, closed early in 1971. That was three years into the Age of the Honda 4, but the Venom Thruxton had been a worthy final torchbearer for the traditional sporting big single, the pinnacle in a long tradition of a certain kind of excellence, living history as well as a damned fine ride.

If the Thruxton's café racer style had looked backward, the only other British roadster 500 of consequence during this decade exemplified what was coming. The

Above: *1968 was the last year for Triumph's trademark parcel rack, following a grisly US lawsuit known at Meriden as 'the caught case'.* **Left:** *1968 Triumph T100 Daytona 500, with improved handling and braking. Finned points cover means aftermarket electronic ignition.*

Fifties' rockers had lived their motorcycling with total involvement, but to a Sixties' market largely made up of young Americans, a bike was often a lifestyle accessory, one kick among the many that became available as the baby boomer youth culture flowered wide open, against a background of increasing affluence. The unit T100 sports 500 Triumph twins suited all this quite well. By 1964 they had lost their hated rear paneling, and they shared styling (and till 1968, electrical problems) with the handsome 650s; but they were significantly lighter, weighing in at just 337lb dry, against a Bonnie's 363lb.

James Dean had blasted about on a pre-unit TR5, and in this tradition, the unit T100 became a happening bike, on both Coasts. In San Francisco one of Janis Joplin's female lovers bought one for her girlfriend, and young dudes could be seen racing up to the Factory in Manhattan on them in Andy Warhol movies. But there were, naturally, hazards to using motorcycles primarily as decoration. Bob Dylan sported a Triumph T-shirt on the cover of his 1965 album *Highway 61 Revisited*, but the next year was said to have suffered head injuries that triggered an eighteen month hiatus in his career, when he came off the twin which his pal Joan Baez said he "sat on like a sack of potatoes".

The 500 Triumph was certainly pretty, but by then was beginning to look badly outclassed by Honda's 450 dohc 'Black Bomber'. Then for 1967 Doug Hele went to work on it in the light of his Daytona race wins with Buddy Elmore in 1966. Elmore had been mounted on the only one of Hele's six race T100s which had survived practice, with an engine that had undergone its sixth major rebuild the night before the race! While Gary Nixon would repeat the victory that year, the production T100, while remaining relatively crude, became an extremely hot motorcycle. They were already good for nearly 100mph in 1966 Tiger 100 form, but handling, despite an additional frame top rail bracing strut for 1965, still suffered from weaving and a light front end at speed. Hele remedied this with a new frame for 1967. It featured an increased diameter downtube and strengthening of the frame top tube so that it, rather than the lower one, became the main load bearer. To redistribute weight the top tube was also shortened, which dropped by half an inch both the overall height and the engine. In addition it provided a 3° steeper steering head angle at 62°, replacing the previous weak 'swan-neck' steering head with a short, fully triangulated lug. At the rear, four years after the 650, a stronger swinging-arm was finally anchored properly by triangular support brackets.

This was as well, because the 500 engine in T100T Daytona form (T100R in the States) now fitted twin carbs on parallel induction tracts but splayed stubs, on a new cylinder head with larger combustion chambers, inlet valves and valve seats, the latter cut deep into the head so as not to disturb combustion. Cams with E3134 forms all round, and a compression ratio of 9.75:1, provided 39bhp at 7,400rpm and a top speed on test of 113mph, much like the Bonnie. The hot 500 engine with its lighter flywheel was peakier,

with a distinct power step at 4,000rpm and another at 6,000. It needed plenty of gearchanging to keep the revs up and the plot on the boil; even with road gearing on the low side, it was good for 88mph in 3rd. There was high-frequency vibration, but the small pistons kept it bearable.

And things got even better. In 1968 the

Left: *The powerful, peaky 1968 Daytona 500 engine with twin Amal Type 900 Concentric carbs, adopted for that year, feeding its redesigned head. 1969 saw the engine further strengthened, with a new end-fed crankshaft running on stronger bearings.*

Above top: *On Triumphs, Smiths speedo and tacho had changed from the Chronometric type to less reliable magnetic ones in 1964.*
Above: *An electrical improvement on this 1968 T100 had been re-siting the Zener diode and its finned heat-sink under the headlamp.*

Daytona got the 8 inch twin-leading shoe brake and a version of the improved, two-way damped front forks. The peak came in 1969 with a redesigned crankshaft layout to bring the bottom end to its ultimate strength. The previous plain timing side bearings had been a weak point on the very rapid T100T, which as on BSA's A65 revealed a potential to turn in their cases and cut off the oil supply to the big ends. It was replaced with a ball journal bearing, and oil to the big ends was fed axially through a

redesigned timing cover into the crankshaft core and thence to the big ends. The external clues were two bumps at the front and rear of the timing chest; those were the motors to have. The 115mph potential, with handling to match, was pretty remarkable in a cooking-based pushrod 500, but save for Those Who Knew, the Daytona never really received the appreciation it deserved, swept over by larger capacities and Japanese refinement and reliability, until finally going under with the Meriden workers sit-in of 1973–74.

1964 Norton Dominator 650SS

Low and purposeful, the no-fuss lines of the traditional 650SS represented British understatement. For in these years, the race-bred Featherbed frame and Roadholder forks allied with the tough and punchy 650 engine to rule the roads. Approach with respect. Silver and black had always been the traditional colors for Norton's racers, so even the look of the bike, with chromed mudguards effortlessly providing the necessary glitter, was appropriate to one of the marque's ultimate roadburners.

Specification

Model
Norton Dominator 650SS
Year
1964
Bore and stroke
68 x 89mm
Displacement
646cc (39.40cu. in.)
Bhp
49 @ 6,800rpm
Top speed
112mph (188kph)
Fuel consumption (overall)
50mpg
Transmission
4-speed
Wheelbase
55.5 in
Wheel and tire dimensions
3.00 x 19in (front); 3.50 x 19in (rear)
Frame type
'Featherbed' duplex downtube cradle
Weight (dry)
398lb (180.5kg)

1969–1975

"THE FINAL CURTAIN"

THE YEAR 1968 had seen the big challenge to Britain as the premier builder of mass market large capacity motorcycles, in the shape of Honda's CB750, its cross-the-frame four cylinder engine the form of the future. But the home industry's demise was not to be primarily from Japanese competition; it was self-inflicted. With US demand at an all-time high, in one newspaper's memorable words, BSA/Triumph "snatched defeat from the jaws of victory".

An entire older generation of management, the 'Forty-year men', including Edward Turner, had stepped down at around the same time in the early Sixties. The new executives, often drafted in from other fields, attempted, to their credit, the

Left: The 1970 T120 Bonneville, a perfected 650 twin only slightly let down by a tank panel layout less attractive than previously. **Below:** *1970 was the Triumph Bonneville's last year in classic form. Practical touches like the ammeter would be gone for 1971.*

modernization of the industry, if not its products. But they did it in a poorly co-ordinated, insensitive and extravagant fashion. BSA/Triumph crashed financially in 1971 and BSA ceased making bikes early in 1972. After an attempted rally, centred on Triumph at Meriden, in 1973 what remained was subject to a government-sponsored merger with Dennis Poore's Norton–Villiers, itself the fruit of Poore's 1966 takeover of AMC. Poore proved himself no less insensitive than his predecessors

and his 1973 announcement of Meriden's closure triggered a sit-in, and after two long years, a workers co-op there. Permanently under-financed and tied to a twin engine design nearly 40 years old in perhaps its least satisfactory, 750 incarnation, they staggered on for another eight years. Meanwhile Poore's own NVT operation had collapsed in 1975, bringing the real end of the old generation of British motorcycles.

So in hindsight there is something of the flame flaring brightest before it dies about the 1969 and 1970 650 Bonnevilles, which in many ways were the best of them all. Already in theory they had been surpassed as Triumph's flagship by the group's answer to the big Honda, the three cylinder 750 Trident. Nevertheless it was on a Bonnie that Percy Tait triumphed in the 1969 Thruxton 500 again, leading home four more of them in the first seven places; and on another that Malcolm Uphill won that year's Production TT at a memorable aver-

age speed of 99.99mph. Quite a finale, before the triples got their turn.

What made the '69 big twins, the T120 and single carb TR6, the best? With the cycle parts virtually sorted, principally it was a final major change within the engine. For 1969 a new crankshaft with a heavier flywheel was fitted. The flywheel, in the words of John Nelson, "applied a 'smoothing' of inertia to the crankshaft ... reducing the peakiness of the engine vibration." New conrods, and pistons with thicker crowns were also fitted. A last improvement finally laid to rest a problem that had dogged the Triumph twin engine from the start, namely rapid wear of their camshafts, particularly the exhaust one. This was now cured by their being treated with the nitriding process. On the cycle side the powerful twin-leading shoe brake had occasionally suffered dangerously when the loop of its operating cable had snagged under the front mudguard and pulled the brake on. For 1969 it was given a

bell-crank forward operating lever, which permitted the cable run to lie parallel to the fork leg and cured the problem.

1970's last major step forward involved revised engine breathing. The timed breather was dispensed with, as the crankcase now breathed directly into the primary chain case, and from there to atmosphere via a new breather elbow bolted to the rear of the crankcase. A useful additional benefit of this system was that the oil level in the primary chaincase was now automatically maintained with no need for additional topping up. There was, however, one retrograde step taken after the beginning of that model year. The gearbox camplate was altered, to a pre-

Below: *The 1970 Triumph Bonneville with its revised engine breathing. The big-bore breather exitting the top rear of the chaincase led to the top left of the rear mudguard. Under the tank nose, that year's twin Windtone horns were the most powerful ever.*

cision pressing operated by a leaf indexing spring. Unsatisfactory in use and very awkward to replace in service, it lingered until mid-1973. But overall, the T120 Bonneville by then was the definitive conventional big twin. A 112mph motorcycle with confidence-inspiring handling, power that came in at tickover and went smoothly up to the maximum, excellent traffic manners and punch at low revs, the perfected Triumph 650 was a good, fast all-rounder.

Then, naturally, they cocked it up, first with 1971's oil-in-frame cycle parts, launched late, with the frames frequently contaminated with swarf, and with a lofty 34½ inch seat height. When that had been

Right: *Since 1969, Triumph rear units had exposed and chromed springs. 1970 was the last year for absorption-type silencers.*
Below: *From 1969, the Triumph twins' petrol tank badge had become this restrained 'picture frame' type.*

sorted out, in 1973 with the T140 they went to a 750 capacity which Hele and Hopwood had always advised against, due to increased vibration. H. and H. had been right, and in addition the engine had to be de-tuned for production, as in full-on form it had snapped its crankshaft. The Bonneville was never the same again. Which left the late Sixties' twins up there in motorcycle heaven. As Peter Egan wrote in *Cycle World*, the '67–'70 Bonnie "seemed, like the DC3 or the Winchester saddle gun, to be the final product and distillation of everything learned about balance and proportion in the era that preceded it."

The 750 capacity was a market necessity, as since 1968 650s had no longer been at the cutting edge, which had begun its irrevocable swing to the East with the Honda 4. And even in the parallel twin world a 750 twin had emerged, one of two final designs from the traditional British industry which would give the Japanese a run for their money before the 1975 collapse. This was Norton's Commando, a precarious but effective solution to the twin's endemic problem of high-speed vibration.

Dennis Poore in 1967 had needed a flagship to launch his new Norton–Villiers operation. At AMC's Plumstead factory which he had taken over, they had already boosted the output of Norton's 750 Atlas to 58bhp. When alternative prototype power plants failed to fulfil expectation, with a Poore-imposed six month deadline to the November '67 Show, the Atlas was pressed into service by the design team to go in the spine frame already laid out for another engine. But that left the problem of Atlas vibration, for at high speed the big Norton twin was an eyeball-blurring shaker. Rubber mounting the engine had already been tried and rejected, but now team head Bernard Hooper hit on the notion of in addition making the swinging-arm pivot on the Norton's still separate gearbox, and then rubber mounting the lot. This would give

Left: *Early Norton Commandos like this 1969 Fastback 750 were a mixture of old and new styles. Familiar 'Roadholder' forks and cigar silencers went with the dualseat with its unusual 'ears' blending into the fiberglass tank and 'fastback' tail unit.*

motorway runs in relative comfort, though the 'sit-on' riding position was not the best.

The new frame, initially still produced entirely at Reynolds Tubes, might not handle as sure-footedly as a Featherbed at high speed, with a slow weave known as 'Commando Creep' setting in above 90 mph, but it was not dangerous (and the chassis was cheaper to produce for the com-

the Chairman his flagship, though it was only intended to be a stopgap model. In fact it would be produced for ten years.

It should not have worked, but it did. The Isolastic mounting system required shimming in every 5,000 miles or so, a tedious job, and unnecessarily so as, from early on, the company had developed an easier-to-use Vernier adjustment design. But the penny-pinching which would blight the model in many ways meant that this was only fitted to the final 1975 models. The job was a necessary one as otherwise the handling suffered – occasionally, after extreme neglect, with fatal consequences. But if the mounts were

Above: The Commando fitted a new twin leading shoe front brake. Better than its predecessor, but not as good as BSA/Triumph's.
Right: The 1969 Commando's rear mountings can be seen behind the gearbox, and its front ones ahead of the contact-breaker housing.

properly set up, though the engine shook about gently at rest and at low speeds up to around 2,500rpm, after that a magical transformation occurred for the rider as vibration just went away. The author went from a 650SS Norton to a 750 Commando, and it was quite a transformation. Here was a twin that could handle long rides and

pany). The machine as a whole was highly rideable. The early 750s were still light at 395lb dry for a '71 Roadster. The separate gearbox meant a cooler running unit and smoother transmission, though a potential drawback was the single diaphragm clutch which could be a heavy pull, and make round-town riding a chore.

The 745cc engine with its unfashionably long stroke at 89mm, kept a lazy, likeable feel to the way the big twin delivered its power (56bhp on early versions). The 750 was good for 115mph and more, with 0-100 in 12 seconds, but its real strength was bottom-end stomp, unbelievable torque right from standstill; the Commando reveled in winding country roads and mountains where both the torque and the excellent handling in its mid-range could be exploited to the full, with the Roadster 'peashooter' silencers giving a lovely crackling roar. A 'Super 7' comparison test in *Cycle* magazine put a Commando up against the Honda-4, Suzuki GT750 and a Kawasaki triple and it came out just about on top; a 12.69 second standing quarter-mile had not hurt. In their best year Norton

would sell 17,000 Commandos on both coasts of America.

The model's styling changed quite radically over the years, since it was soon Norton's only motorcycle, and they offered it in many guises. Connoisseurs often rate the early Fastback variants as favorite, though the '72-on Roadsters and Interstates were the major-ity models. Perhaps more than any other British twin the Commando suffered from Good Bike/Bad Bike syndrome, and another reason for rating the Fastback from 1968–69 in particular, was that then it was still being built at Plumstead, with know-how which was lost when Poore in 1970 moved assembly to Andover, where labour was 'green' and the engines had to be trucked down from the old Villiers factory at Wolverhampton, where they were now made.

Andover was the scene of the Great Combat Engine Disaster of 1972, when Poore, to cover the price rise necessary to finance that year's new front disc brake, insisted that the 750 engine should simulta-

neously be offered in hot, 10:1 compression Combat form, with a claimed output of 65 bhp. This regularly knocked out the main bearings in less than 5,000 miles. Rapid return to a lower state of tune plus a 'Superblend' replacement bearing soon dealt with the problem, and the last 750 models so equipped were probably the best of all. But

Left: *The 1969 Commando 750 Fastback appealed to many with its racer styling. The cable-operated rear brake was a weak point.*
Above: *The Commando was a long bike, and only later handlebar bends would give a comfortable position for fast riding.*

the Commando's street cred, which had led it to be voted Machine of the Year by *Motor Cycle News* readers five times running, never recovered from the episode. The big Nortons had won the Thruxton 500, but the heroic Commando-based John Player Norton F750 race effort also went down soon after that, though not before Peter Williams had won the 1973 Isle of Man

Formula 750 race. The marque's sporting honor was then confined to the Californian flat tracks and the winning Axtell-tuned Ron Wood Nortons.

Meanwhile in the face of the new street-beating Kawasaki Z900, Norton upped the road bikes to 850 capacity; actually 829cc, done by taking the 750's 73mm bore out to 77mm. 850 weight crept up – a '74 Inter-state was 430lb dry – and the smoothing effect of the Isolastics came in a little later, at

Below: *Every detail of the new Norton had been carefully considered, including its racy snap-top fuel cap. The very earliest 1968 Commandos had a circular tank badge.*

around 3,000rpm, with the bigger motor. With noise emission laws now a consideration, top speeds began to fall, and the 850 took longer to get to them. But with the Superblend bearings as standard and stronger crankcases, cylinder barrels and gearboxes, 850s were more reliable – at least if you got a good one.

For production of the whole bike had moved up to Wolverhampton during 1973, and manufacturing conditions up there were often of the 'dark satanic mills' variety. For instance, quite startling variations in Commando handling from around that time may be partly explained by the fact that the cash-conscious company had starting sourcing some of the frames in Italy. These proved to vary considerably in quality, and at the rough-and-ready Wolverhampton plant, in Quality Control if the 'acceptance gauge', a blunt lump of metal meant to go loosely through the steering head, did not fit, the inspector was in the habit of hammering it through until it did!

Commando performance continued to fall off with the 1974 Mk IIA 850 which featured quieter 'bean-can' silencers to meet new European noise requirements, though in fact it was not the silencers but the more restrictive large plastic bafflebox containing the air cleaners and suppressing induction roar which was the culprit. But the intake 'ears' at the bottom end of the airbox were detachable, and once removed, restored the power levels. The Mk IIA was not too heavy at 410lb dry in the Roadster version, and with a little work could achieve remarkable levels of performance. It exemplified how a core of extremely dedicated engineers at Wolverhampton continued to patiently develop the big Norton and strove to iron out its kinks.

One of them was John Baker of the Experimental Dept. Baker was responsible for the preparation of fellow employee Dave Rawlins' drag bikes. On a slightly modified Mk IIA Rawlins ran an 11.53 standing quarter at MIRA, and for 1974 held all the Street

Right: *The 1974 Commando 850 Mk IIA had come a long way since the early Fastback. A beefy bike with a disc brake between its forks, its rakish lines ran from the tilt of the barrels to the angle of the rear suspension.*

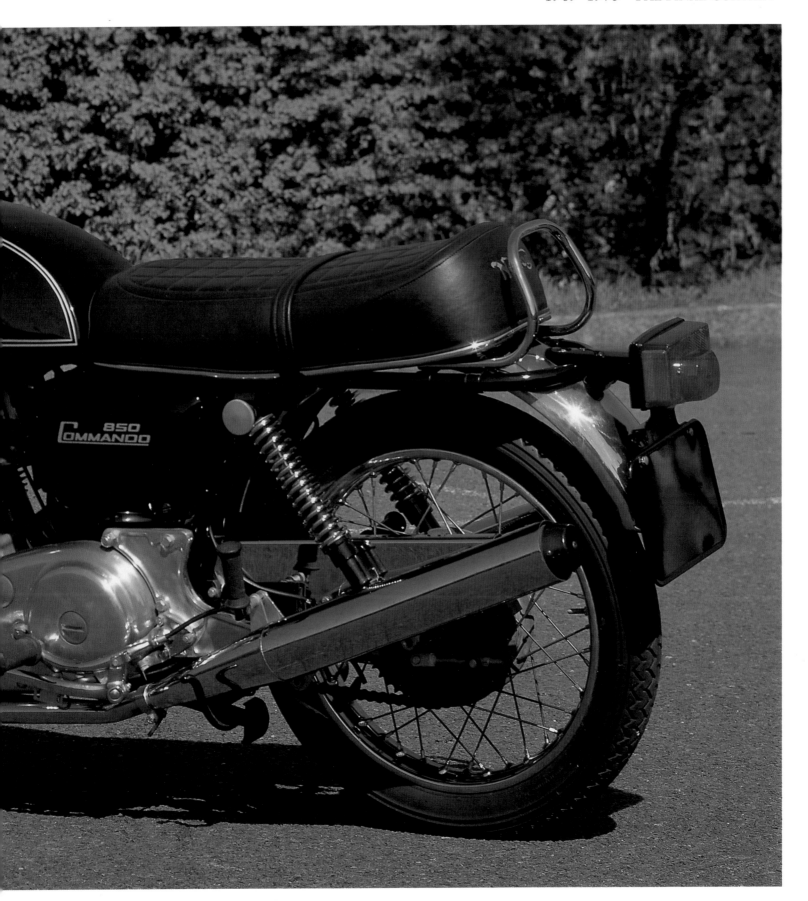

Bike titles at Santa Pod, Britain's top strip, with an elapsed time of 12 seconds dead. Some of the developments which had made this possible had been passed on to the Mk IIA production machines. The dragster's profiled inlet ports took 34mm carbs and then tapered to 32mm; on the production bike this was replicated with stock 32mm carbs and the ports tapering to 30mm, which restored the 850's vital mid-range power between 3,000 and 4,000rpm.

Previous Interstates had been criticized for their massive 5¼ gallon petrol tank being impractically wide at the rear. The Mk IIA's had a section removed from its center and was not such an uncomfortable stretch between the rider's knees. At 4.5 gallons some capacity had been lost, but since this 850 still returned around 50 miles to the gallon, it still gave useful range. The model also fitted narrower 'Majorca' handlebars and a cross-hatched seat cover, useful in preventing the rider slipping backward under hard acceleration, and with deeper padding. The 850 frame's steering head angle had been increased by 1° to the ubiquitous 62°, with the forks brought back to increase the trail yet retain the 750's wheelbase, and this helped counter the tendency to lightness at the front end at speed. In combination with the excellent roadholding this meant that the big ones could be chucked around in a highly satisfying manner.

The Mk IIA's gearing was raised slightly overall as well as specifically in 2nd gear by changing the pinions in the gear cluster, because the European noise test had required acceleration in 2nd. The result of the raise was a slight loss of tractability in top as well as less comfortable town riding, but the trade-off was ratios now just right for fast open riding. And gearing could always be changed; Dave Rawlins raised his with a 24-tooth sprocket, took a carefully assembled and run-in stock Mk IIA using the available Sports kit with its SS cam and 10:1 compression pistons, lowered the rid-

Left: *Double pin-striping on the tank marked the 850s. Twin 32mm Amal Concentrics were standard on all Commandos. Under the big touring tank lay the duplex downtube frame's massive spine. The 850's 4-speed AMC gearbox had been strengthened.*

Above: *By 1974, the Commando 850 Mk IIA's engine break-in period was already an anachronism, as Oriental bikes did not need it.*
Right: *The 850 Mk IIA's annular discharge silencers, known as 'black caps' or 'bean cans', were not restrictive, but the new airbox was.*

ing position, and was clocked at over 142mph. The standard bike's top end was a respectable but no longer sensational 110mph, but even with the taller gearing, that practical, meaty mid-range acceleration was still its strongest point.

The final 850 Mk III for 1975, with ineffective electric start and many other changes was by now well overweight at 466lb dry, and was marketed by NVT primarily as a tourer, which is what it was. But in their heyday the Commandos had been a fast, usable and highly likeable final variant of the Big Twin.

BSA/Triumph meanwhile had gone down another route by creating what in some terms was a twin with an extra cylinder, sometimes described as 'a Tiger-and-a-half'. But the dimensions involved in the 740cc BSA Rocket 3/Triumph T150 Trident triples were not modular ones deriving from the cylinder dimensions of the current Triumph 500 twin, the Daytona; that would have made too much sense. But they were the same as BSA/Triumph's current 250 single; there had been a modular intention, but it had got lost

Left: *BSA's version of the triple had its cylinders inclined forward. The reflectors were set in caps on the end of the oil cooler.*
Above: *The BSA Rocket 3 Mk I today simply looks like a chunky roadburner with a funny silencer. In 1969 it seeemed dauntingly odd.*

in the prolonged development period. Similarly, there was the apparently barmy decision to release the triple in two quite different versions, which meant the constant interruption of an already complicated engine manufacturing process at BSA's Small Heath works, where the motors for both were built. But complex inter-company politics had decreed that it should be so – even if that limited initial production to a mere 3,500 a year of each, which could not be profitable at a time when profit was badly needed, and which pushed their price up beyond what could be successful commercially.

The engines featured a one-piece crankshaft with a 120° throw so that each piston reached the top of its stroke in turn, providing excellent primary balance and basic smoothness, though the latter was sometimes marred by other factors. By providing bobweights instead of flywheels, and positioning the alternator unconventionally on the right end of the crankshaft, the engine's overall

width, a design problem for Hopwood and Hele, was admirably held down to just 3½ inches more than a Bonneville.

The basic engine layout, with fore and aft gear-driven camshafts operating vertical pushrods in tubes located in between the cylinders, was as on the Triumph twin. Unfortunately lack of cash for new production machinery meant that the crankcases still had to be vertically rather than horizontally split, a traditionally leak-prone arrangement. The 4-speed gearbox was built in unit with the engine. Despite the use of alloy for both the barrels and the one-piece cylinder head casting, the triple engine was heavy at 180lb, and all-up weight was 468lb – exactly

the same for both versions, the company claimed. Both fitted an oil cooler as standard, since the triple's oil circulated 3.5 times as fast as on the twins, and the big engine's plain bearings caused oil temperature to rise.

The BSA version of this engine had its barrels tilted forward 15°, which was the sexier look chosen as the basis for the Vetter-styled limited edition factory custom X75 Hurricane, though by the time it emerged in 1973, BSA had gone down and it had to be badged a Triumph. The Trident opted for a more traditional upright look, and the outline of its gearbox was kept plainly visible, chiming with the unit twins. It ran in a single downtube frame, while the Rocket 3 chose the duplex downtube layout favored by BSA. There was little to chose between the handling, though an Owners' Report thought the BSA had a slight edge.

The slab-sided styling on both the first versions looked odd to late Sixties eyes. It had been turned over to the Ogle styling studio, chiefly remembered in automotive terms as responsible for the Reliant Robin 3-wheeler, the 'plastic pig'. The Ogle concepts had been further reworked by the BSA/Triumph R & D establishment at Umberslade Hall. The BSA version was initially the more attractive, in a substantial way. Its polychromatic red paint compared well with the early Triumph's watery Aquamarine finish. The 'Flash Gordon' ray-gun silencers on both with their triple tail pipes, might seem bizarre, but to Hele the point was that they "had sufficient volume to accommodate the very successful reverse flow element that we had made sure was inside." They also gave a lovely wail on a

Right: *The badge on the Rocket 3's steering damper reminded you which triple you owned. Instruments were Smiths Magnetic.*
Below: *The Rocket 3's 'ray-gun' silencers were striking. They would prove to give the best performance of any fitted to the triples.*

rising throttle, though the full throat version of this was reserved for the racers. American Triumph dealers were deeply disappointed with the early Tridents as previous prototypes had been styled like conventional Triumph twins with rounded tanks, cylindrical silencers, etc. Texas dealer Jack Wilson affirmed "We couldn't give those '69 Tridents away they were so ugly." And when Triumph hastily came up with an early 1970 'beauty kit' for the US to convert them, Wilson pounded 30 of the previous slab-sided tanks flat with a sledge-hammer.

Ill-advised looks were not to be the triples' only problem. Once again poor quality control at factory level in the low morale of the day meant wide variations in the motorcycles. An early bout of badly misaligned triplex primary chains due to out-of-line chainwheels was traced to a Small Heath worker trying to boost his piecework earnings by putting up to six chainwheels on the broaching machine at a time. Bad high-speed vibration was discovered by Hele to be down to the factory having speeded up the crankshaft machining process, plunge-grinding the crankshafts without thought for the consequences, which resulted in bobweights of uneven thickness and altered balance factors. Other troubles included temperamental triple contact breakers leading to wandering ignition timing, fuel consumption that could drop below 30mpg, a diaphragm clutch that gave barely enough lift, short-life rubbers in the clutch sprockets' cush drive, extremely fiddly tappet adjustment, clattering valves, rapid wear valve guides leading to smoking exhausts and high oil consumption, oil leaks, and porous castings. Yet most of these problems, though irritating, were peripheral rather than fundamental, and factory service personnel confirm that the triples were considerably more reliable than the contemporary twins.

That they could be storming performers was shortly confirmed round race-tracks on both sides of the Atlantic. Despite a flawed 1970 debut at Daytona due to teething troubles, BSA/Triumph triples took the first 5 places in that year's American racing championship series; initially in the States the BSA outsold the Trident, partly because of a well-publicized record breaking session, as well as more frequent AMA road race victories, including Dick Mann's 1971 Daytona win. Malcolm Uphill won the 1970 Production TT, and Tom Dickie with Paul Smart won the Bol D'Or endurance production race, with Percy Tait coming in 5th on an oil-soaked Trident, the legendary Slippery Sam, which would go on to win the following 5 Production TT's. For the works F750 racers with frames by Rob North, highlights would include John 'Mooneyes'

Below: *The Rocket 3 would be the last truly new model from Small Heath. Internal politics meant that it was pushed hard at the time, but floored by production constraints.*

Above: *The outrageously tarty BSA Rocket 3 Mk II, part of the 1971 range which helped finish off the marque.*
Left: *The triples shone in production racing. Here David Nixon refuels the Boyer Trident he took to 3rd place in the 1972 Thruxton 500.*

Cooper on a Rocket 3 at the '71 Mallory Park Race of the Year beating Agostini on the full house MV500 overhead cam racer, and then just scooping the US Formula 750 at Ontario Raceways, California. So the triples provided an incredible finale for British four-stroke pushrod power before racing became dominated from 1973 onward by Japanese two-strokes.

The road bikes too brought performance that had not been seen since the big Vincent. 125mph top speeds, 12.78 standing quarters, strong mid-range acceleration from 80 to 110mph – in the early Seventies, this was a true superbike. However, Trident rider comfort was not good due to footrests set too far forward and a seat which subsided. The handling was good and forgiving rather than superlative – initially *Cycle World* had found the T150 'cumbersome' after the Bonneville, but though a *Cycle* 1970 Super 7 test preferred the Commando, it put the Trident's handling 2nd out of the seven machines. The twin-leading shoe drum front brake, good as it was, was glaringly inadequate for the triple's weight and performance – one American magazine described it as "like pasting an airmail stamp on your duff and pre-addressing yourself to Saint Peter". The engine's fundamental strength was emphasized by the way in which the racers used standard con rods for a whole season, and standard crankshafts which were reground at the end of each season and then used again.

The BSAs underwent a flamboyant restyle for 1971. In common with almost all the group's machines, Tridents included, they fitted modern-looking, redesigned cast-alloy front forks, with damping by clack valve rather than the previous shuttle valve. Pivoting on taper-roller steering head bearings, the forks performed well and provided over 6 inches of movement. But their hard-chromed stanchions were exposed and ungaitered and this vulnerable arrangement with its rapid wear for the fork oil seals, set the tone of the infamous BSA/Triumph '71 range – style got precedence over practicality. The range represented the outer edge of the motorcycle-as-plaything philosophy.

Above the forks, flat-back headlamps were carried on spindly, shaped brackets of chromed steel rod. These proved fracture-prone, as were the similar thin wire stays for the impractically small chromed front mudguards. The shock absorbers' chromed springs were also now fully exposed. Direction indicators might have looked modern, but the ones fitted to the range were chromed plastic jobs from Lucas with a habit of rotating skyward and malfunctioning, and were operated by awkward thumb switches vulnerable to the wet. At a time when a disc brake was a must, if only to counter the big Honda, new conical-hub drum brakes were fitted, less effective than their predecessors. And handlebars were a wildly impractical 33 inches in width.

The Mk II BSA topped that year's T150 Trident in the fantasy league by featuring, along with the rest of the benighted '71 range from Small Heath, a pale Dove Gray finish for its frame and stands – not a good idea on any traditional British bike. The Rocket 3 was also topped off with a tiny 2¾ gallon petrol tank, finished in

Right: *The BSA/Triumph alloy conical hub twin leading shoe front brake could be made to work quite well but a disc was really needed.*
Below: *High and wi-i-ide, the 1971 Rocket 3 certainly had pizazz. Note the oil cooler protruding on each side of the minimal tank.*

Flamboyant Red or Blue, with chromed panels and the pear-shaped anodized light alloy tank badges off the previous twins. The Trident's conventional rounded tank also shared the same low capacity. Given the triple's thirst this was impractical in the extreme, but the sheer chutzpah of the Rocket 3 Mk II's styling has to evoke a grudging admiration in anyone reared on *Easy Rider.* Back in reality, a combination of new circular air cleaners, shapelier but more restrictive megaphone silencers, altered throttle slides, a compression drop plus slightly lower gearing, meant that both triples were down on previous power levels

Right: *'Born to be Wild.' The 1971 Rocket 3 Mk II, outrageous and impractical, nevertheless emphasized the good job that designers Hele and Hopwood had done in keeping the three-cylinder power plant admirably narrow and compact.*

and top speed, though their mid-range response was improved.

The Rocket 3 went back to a conventional look for their last year. Trident production struggled on through the group collapse and the NVT merger, acquiring a 5-speed gearbox during 1972, which with new 'cigar' silencers and a 10 inch Lockheed front disc brake, formed the basis of the more conventionally styled T150V, though UK variants still had the slab-sided tank. With the Meriden sit-in, manufacture of the Trident had to be transferred entirely to Small Heath, meaning a six month gap in production. After a year's output of the T150V, the final Trident was launched in the UK in March 1975.

This was the T160. Its engine had originally been intended to be an 850, the long-stroke 'Thunderbird III', but with NVT battling Meriden, that was not to be. It was however the best of the lot for handling, with the frame not the Rob North F750

type, but still race-bred via the works production racers. Its lower front tubes were raised to improve ground clearance; shorter forks, still pivoting on taper roller steering head bearings, were mounted at a familiar 62° angle; and the engine's weight had been shifted significantly, partly via cylinders angled forward in the Rocket 3 style but at 12° in this instance, and partly by the engine being moved 1/2 an inch forward and 1 inch higher. The result was outstanding handling. Like a real thoroughbred, the harder it was pushed the better it responded. Despite weight now standing at a whopping 503lb dry, there was a new nimbleness, with well-matched suspension meaning that the T160

Below: *The final triple, Triumph's T160 Trident had originally been intended as an 850. With a race-bred frame, electric starter behind its inclined cylinders and sinuous three-into-four-into-two exhaust system, it was the last and best of the old triples.*

could be cornered just as hard as you liked.

Part of the weight came from an electric starter, mounted in the area behind the cylinders freed up by the forward-tilted barrels; though the kickstart was retained, at least the Trident's electric foot worked better than the Commando's. Other new features included a disc brake at the rear, and both it and the front one now performed better in the wet. The gearchange had shifted to the left, in line with US legislation. There was an improved clutch shock absorber, a longer-wearing duplex primary drive chain, and increased lift for the clutch. Tappet adjustment was also now easier. The riding position had been greatly improved, though the seat was still too squashy. Sadly there were also still plenty of production niggles, such as high oil consumption from piston ring problems and even oval bores, as well as unsatisfactory Lucas electrical switchgear. A high price was another minus point.

The triple's styling however had finally

cohered in the T160, starting with a really shapely petrol tank, in Cherokee Red with gold-lined white flashes and tank badges picked out in white, or in white with gold-lined Sunflower Yellow flashes, in either 4.8 or 3.7 gallon capacities. With the gearing lowered a little, and a restrictive airbox plus versions of the NVT 'bean-can' silencers, top speed was down at around 117mph. But it is impossible to overemphasize what a responsive, rapid yet secure-feeling delight riding a T160 proved to be. Production ended all too soon after that with the NVT collapse, in 1976. But the T160 Trident represents a fitting end to twenty-five years that had produced some great British motorcycles.

Right: *Overdue modern features on the T160 Trident included its 10 inch Lockheed disc brakes, both front, and, as seen here, rear.*
Below: *Though badged Triumph, NVT's industrial strife with Triumph's Meriden home meant that T160s were built at Small Heath.*

1975 Triumph T160 Trident

The T160 Trident represented the last flowering of the old British motorcycle industry. Its handsome looks – every inch a Triumph, even if it was built at the old BSA factory – powerful performance and truly excellent race-bred handling made it an appropriate candidate.

Specification

Model
Triumph T160 Trident
Year
1975
Bore and stroke
67 x 70 mm
Displacement
740cc (45.14cu. in.)
Bhp
58 @ 7,250rpm
Top speed
117mph (188kph)
Fuel consumption (overall)
36.5mpg
Transmission
5-speed
Wheelbase
58in
Wheel and tire dimensions
4.10 x 19in (front) ; 4.10 x 19in (rear)
Frame type
Single downtube cradle
Weight (dry)
503lb (229kg)

INDEX